Parish Ministry
for Maturing
Adults

Principles, Plans,

& Bold Proposals

PARISH MINISTRY
for
MATURING ADULTS

PRINCIPLES, PLANS, & BOLD PROPOSALS

Richard P. Johnson

TWENTY
THIRD 23rd
PUBLICATIONS

Twenty-Third Publications
A Division of Bayard
One Montauk Avenue, Suite 200
New London, CT 06320
(860) 437-3012 or (800) 321-0411
www.23rdpublications.com

ISBN 978-1-58595-621-0
Library of Congress Catalog Card Number: 2006936869
Printed in the U.S.A.

In memory of
Father Bob Chenoweth
Catholic priest and lifelong friend to all,
especially maturing adults.

I dedicate this book to all those
whose hearts are moved by
the marvelous God-given gift of aging;
who can look into the eyes
of a spiritually maturing adult
and see a reflection of Jesus Christ.
I say a prayer of thanksgiving
for their steadfastness, patience,
compassion, understanding, simplicity,
hope, wisdom, empathy, and drive.

Table of Contents

Introduction

A true crisis exists in the field of religion and aging.
Almost no thorough or extensive research is being done
to better understand how spiritual resources and reli-
gious life contribute to successful adult development,
nor how it interacts with other variables in later life.
(James J. Seeber, *Spiritual Maturity in the Later Years*)

The current "true crisis" in parish ministry for maturing adults is the reason I've written this book. My goal here is that readers will use it as both a handbook and a reference and that everyone involved in parish ministry for maturing adults will keep it by their side for both inspiration and motivation.

What we need now more than ever is to become more intentional in our work to, with, and for maturing adults. We can and must become more active, more assertive, and more focused on the fundamentals of ministering to those in their maturing years. A new vision of this ministry will include an advancing appreciation for this later time of life as having immense spiritual purpose: that this time of life is specially designed by God to bring people ever closer to both God and their true selves. Spiritual development never stops but

> **As we mature our spiritual pace quickens.**

intensifies as people move through the years. All of us can learn to truly see aging as a gift from God!

As I look into the future, I see this ministry growing steadily and surely. I see it taking its rightful place among other parish ministries; indeed, I see it becoming the fastest growing ministry in the Church over the next twenty years. I see armies of spiritually maturing adults rising up as a renewing force for good in our culture. I see them taking on deeper and broader roles in our Church and in our community. I see a deeper understanding of the aging process taking hold in the hearts and minds of spiritually maturing adults—an understanding that will lead to greatly expanded opportunities for helping others and acts of compassion.

Beyond service, I see spiritually maturing adults rising to take on mentor roles where they become true sages and wisdom figures and where they can point to new horizons by remembering both the successes and the mistakes of the past. Still further beyond wisdom, I see spiritually maturing adults emerging as leaders in prayer, in corporal and spiritual works of mercy, and in the practice of virtue. I see all of this and more.

For these things to happen, our maturing adult members need the support of their Church perhaps in a different way than in previous life stages. They need the nurturance of care and compassion, the understanding of their real needs as they are now, the necessary help in discerning the call of God today, the encouragement to continue their spiritual pilgrimage, and the direction to reach out to others in new ways. Our Church needs to be "fully with" its maturing children and not stand idly by as they drift away—perhaps not in body, but certainly in mind and soul—devoid of purpose or direction, living unsatisfying lives of diversion, personal uncertainty, and spiritual stagnation.

For all these reasons, we need a new vision for parish ministry with maturing adults, and we need to move beyond social activities alone to a new model of spiritual growth and personal development—one that adds vitality and vibrancy to the lives of older parishioners. The time has come for us in the Catholic Church to adopt this new model and to embrace the true meaning of aging and the senior years.

I hope you find this book encouraging and inspiring. I hope it will motivate you to find and pursue your own unique ministry among spiritually maturing adults. I can think of very few human endeavors that offer more potential fulfillment and personal growth. It is my hope that you become captivated by this holy task and find personal transformation every day of your life!

CHAPTER ONE

The Challenge

I am convinced that the vitality of our parishes and the Church's capacity to fulfill its mission of proclaiming the reign of God are dependent on a refocusing of our energy and resources to the ongoing faith life of adults. (Jane E. Regan, Ph.D., *Toward an Adult Church*)

We are in the first act of a drama that is transforming our culture and changing our Church in ways we have yet to imagine. Unlike any drama before, the opening scene was hardly noticed, yet it has intensified year by year until now, when it's about to take center stage in our faith communities. I'm speaking, of course, about the fact that in one century our longevity has increased by thirty years!

This change has come so fast that it can even be considered sudden—though ninety years is but the blink of an eye in the history of humankind. While God is the prime mover of this profound change, certainly many human communities—including the medical, educational, and public health communities—are all gloves on the hand of God that have contributed to this cultural transformation.

We are just now beginning to experience the consequences of this change. Certainly our financial systems, medical health industries, and care-giving institutions are worried. How will they meet the

> Age is not a thief in the night; no, aging is the master teacher of life.

needs of this escalating number of older adults? The real question, however, is not how they can meet the needs but rather: Will they listen? The same question applies in our parishes. Will we listen to the accumulated wisdom of our maturing adults, or will we simply remove them from center stage? This is a challenging question, even a frightening one, because it demands that we look carefully at our beliefs about aging.

We live in a culture that suffers from age prejudice. It's not that we don't like old people; on an individual level we may have deep respect and great admiration for a particular older person. On a societal level, however, we tend to fear aging, mistrust it, and think of it as a "thief in the night." This is unfortunate because aging is one of the few things that every living person does every single day. Even the Church suffers from ageism.

Yet, the number of maturing adults occupying our church pews increases weekly. This phenomenon will likely continue for at least the next thirty years; indeed, it's likely to remain a permanent fixture in the demographics of our church communities.

According to the *Statistical Yearbook of the Church*, the Church's worldwide-recorded membership at the end of 2004 was 1,098,366,000, or approximately 1 in 6 of the world's population. According to canon law, members are those who have been baptized in, or have been received into, the Catholic Church on making a profession of faith, provided they have not formally renounced membership.

> Our chronological age is the most inaccurate and crude measurement of our value, our accomplishments, and our spirit.

The truth is we don't know how to minister to our older members, and that's why so many parishes and dioceses have offered only social activities and diversions. Groups called Daytimers, Daytrippers, and Bygoners focus solely on what I've come to call "buses, bingo, and brownies." Certainly socialization is important for maturing adults, but there is so much more we can offer. I don't think socialization was what Jesus had in mind when he commanded Peter to "feed my sheep."

Maturing adults have arrived at a time when they can more fully discern the presence of Christ in their lives. They have arrived at a place where inner issues of the heart and soul take on new meaning, a place where a new vision of life can emerge with passionate spiritual vigor, something heretofore unknown in their lives. They need real "soul food" and can now appreciate it with a connoisseur's palate.

What This Ministry Involves

Ministry to maturing adults means different things to different people. Some see it strictly as offering fun and games. Others point to community-related issues, emphasizing the sharing and solving of day-to-day problems. Still others restrict it to Bible study or cultural education or travel opportunities. Actually it's all these things, but it could be so much more.

Spiritual development opportunities for maturing adults succeed when they relate specifically and individually to the *person* of the senior, the special person, the unique child of God. Spiritual development opportunities for maturing adults must deal with issues of *everyday living* in the modern world and hopefully provide greater clarity and guidance on how to live more fully as a follower of Christ. They need to address the social issues of peace and justice, the fundamental interaction of care and compassion, and the over-arching spiritual issues of prayer, good will, wholeness, and compassion.

Clearly, this is the least developed of all parish ministries. This is possibly because when we think of others as "seniors," an unfortunate shift in our thinking takes place: we somehow think that they can now take care of their own spiritual development. Such thinking is driven by our own ignorance that spiritual growth, indeed all positive growth, only happens at younger ages, and further, that "senior" means not adaptable, unable to learn, and not needing further spiritual development.

When the first senior groups were forming in our parishes, cultural attitudes about aging, maturation, and ongoing spiritual formation were very different than they are today. Previously, anyone over the age of sixty-five was seen as "old." Old meant "over-the-hill." Old people had already "done their thing." Not only were their best years behind them, but indeed their real life was behind them as well.

Today we have an entirely new attitude about maturation. We've learned so much from the older adults who continue to live vital and vibrant lives. These are not just the exceptions, the lucky few; they have become the rule. Some older adults not only continue to live vibrant lives, but also push into new territories of personal and spiritual development. The entire definition of

> In the last 100 years, our longevity has increased thirty years! This fact has just begun to evoke responses—socially, culturally, and spiritually.

what it means to be "older" has been dramatically changed with head-spinning speed. And this is only the beginning.

What then is the *new* mission of parish ministry to maturing adults (or whatever it is called in your parish) now? Certainly, the community/social aspect must not be abandoned; social gatherings are valuable and serve to build a strong foundation of Christian care. Yet we need a broader vision, a new agenda, new goals, and a revised mission. Maturing adults are prime for new spiritual development opportunities and genuinely desire to reach their spiritual potential.

CHAPTER TWO

Spiritually Maturing Adults

Who exactly are spiritually maturing adults? While there's no strict dividing age that gives definition to who is and who is not a "maturing adult," one thing is certain; they are not one group. There have been many designations for separate sub-groups, but for my purposes here, I divide them into three separate, but not altogether distinct groups: Boomers (ages fifty-five to seventy-two), Builders (ages seventy-three and above), and Elders (those who live very long lives). Elders often includes the physically and/or cognitively impaired, but it also includes those considered (by Native Americans, for example) to be the wisest members of the community.

Boomers

We can think of Boomers as generally beginning in the mid-fifties and extending through the mid-seventies. For those in the middle class and above, this has been referred to as the "Third Age" of life, a time when people are generally freer to devote themselves more directly to interests, talents, and skills of their own choosing. Whereas retirement is generally

> It's not what age does to us, but what we do with age that marks us as wise or foolish.

a part of the mature middle-aged phase of life, it doesn't necessarily have to be. Certainly, healthy Boomers do not view retirement as a time of decline, diminishment, or even rest. Rather, this stage of life development is best seen as a time of growth, challenging (in a positive way), stimulating, engaging, and participatory; a valuable time when they can explore the world, look more deeply at themselves, and investigate their faith in ways previously unavailable because of full-time work responsibilities.

Much has been written about the uniqueness of this age group, but suffice it to say that Boomers are different than previous generations. They are in better physical shape, are more highly educated, and have greater quality-of-life expectations. Again, unlike any previous generation, their global worldview has been greatly shaped by mass media, technological advances, and world travel. Boomers are generally more affluent than their parents and are said to be reconfiguring the nature of work, family, and retirement. They are certainly poised to extend the former boundaries of "middle age." They have divorced in significantly greater numbers and percentages than any previous generation and consequently, live in family configurations sometimes referred to as blended, mended, bended, or simply ended. Yet Boomers are curious of mind and restless of spirit and are delving into different philosophical and religious ideas. They are hungry for "soul food."

Builders

Builders are even harder to define than Boomers. This stage of life begins around the mid-seventies and its distinguishing factor is a general physical slowing down. Builders' minds may be just as sharp and quick as always, but they suffer some physical diminishment in strength, speed, and stamina that interferes with their activity levels.

Some in this age group remember the Great Depression; all felt its effects, heard first-hand stories of loss and sadness. They either participated in World War II or grew up in its shadow. They were psychologically affected by these two cataclysmic events and carry an amalgam of sometimes contradictory values, including thrift and extravagance, defensiveness and assertiveness, problem solving and passivity, toleration and dissention, acceptance and rejection, and fear and courage. Builders are the generation that laid more cornerstones at churches and parochial schools than any previous generation. They constructed the federal highway system and moved to the suburbs. They are filled with hope of new life. Above all, they want to get things done. They want decisions made and plans executed with abbreviated discussion and little observed sentiment.

These two groups, while overlapping in so much, are still quite different. Naturally, they have much to learn from one another, but the Boomers don't like being identified with the Builders, and the Builders may not feel entirely comfortable with Boomers. Both of these two sub-groups of spiritually maturing adults require human, psychological, and spiritual growth opportunities at the very highest levels. Even though the type and mix of growth opportunities might differ somewhat, the overall need for greatly expanded spiritual growth opportunities applies to both groups.

Boomers are poised to become the largest concentrated age grouping that our culture has ever experienced. The "baby boomers" were born between 1946 and 1964, so they will be the largest segment of the population for years to come! The ranks of Builders have been swelling for years as well. In fact, the greatest percentage of growth in our country is among persons who are eighty-five and older! It's not at all uncommon today to have several centenarians in every parish community!

Elders

"Elders" is the name I give to those maturing adults in the parish who have experienced some form of physical or cognitive debilitation. As a consequence, many in this group require special assistance or personal care. They may be homebound but living alone. They may live with an adult child, or have around-the-clock home care. They may reside in an assisted living facility, or they may have serious enough debilitation that they require full skilled residential care, or what we used to call nursing home care.

Many Elders are unable to come to the parish for educational classes or to participate in the social or outreach programs the parish sponsors. They are simply too impaired. They are the folks who are visited by extraordinary ministers with communion. They are also the ones who may receive services from other maturing adults in the parish. However, it would be a mistake to assume that Elders are merely *recipients* of care. They still have a vocation or ministry, including ministries of prayer, presence, mourning, and celebration. Elders have much to give; they have advanced wisdom, and they have experienced the unique handiwork of God in their lives. They might need our care, but we need their wisdom. We must listen—and listen well—to our elders.

A Negative Connotation

Our culture actually seems to be afraid of aging. Older

adults are often referred to in the media as "the elderly," implying that all maturing adults are somehow decrepit, frail, confused, or worse, certainly a condition to avoid. Unfortunately, many older people have started to identify with this description. This distorted view considers aging to be a senseless physical process of decline that can somehow be defeated or beaten back, a process that makes people feel threatened and helpless.

Aging is, in fact, a progressive force ordained by God that teaches us how to be more authentic. We can be spiritually transformed by aging when we embrace it for all it has to offer and engage fully in the process. Aging is like a spiritual mentor. An Elder is a person whose personality is transformed because she or he sees beyond the physical level of life. An Elder is in touch with the most noble parts of life in ways she or he couldn't have been in younger years. An Elder knows in a simple but profound way that she or he is a child of God.

Current research of the adult life cycle and human growth and development is now shedding new light on the growth potential of spiritually maturing adults. What we're finding is exciting and energizing. Incredibly, research indicates that maturing adults may require more change, more growth, and more personal development in their senior years than they did at any other time in their lives. There are two reasons for this.

First, maturing adults gradually experience a new freedom from societal, career, and familial accountability. This new freedom in and of itself can usher in new perspectives, new thinking, and a new view of themselves. Routine ways of

> We need a new vision of faith-formation for maturing adults, a vastly expanded vision that includes body, mind, and spirit.

thinking, feeling, choosing, and acting are prime for change. The real question here is whether these changes will continue to be shaped solely by secular forces, or whether, and to what degree, the local parish will take an active role.

Second, maturing adults experience more losses than at any previous life stage. Adult developmentalists are discovering that loss can best be seen as behavioral change stimulators. In most cases, when loss is properly framed and compassionately understood, it enhances rather than inhibits interior growth and development.

What is the response of the Church to both this time of new freedom and this time of losses? To what degree will it be there for its maturing adults, not only soothing and consoling them, but also offering them encouragement and providing spiritual growth opportunities? Let's look at the possibilities in more detail.

CHAPTER THREE

Guiding Principles: 1-6

This chapter identifies and describes the essential guiding principles of parish ministry for maturing adults and will look at six of them in some detail. Chapter Four will examine the remaining six. Principles are the ideas that matter most in times of transition; they empower us and clear our vision so we can see where change is needed. Principles are invaluable because they provide a vocabulary for energizing needed activity. So, upon what bedrock beliefs do we base our work with maturing adults? What concepts give us the framework for best discerning a new vision? Here are twelve key principles.

1. Parish ministry for maturing adults pays attention to three dimensions of growth: spiritual, psychological, and physical.

2. Parish ministry for maturing adults should be part of the parish plan, well organized, and consistent in offering services that people will come to count on.

3. Parish ministry for maturing adults employs styles of teaching and learning unique to the people being served.

4. Parish ministry for maturing adults is based on the idea that God is calling each maturing adult in the parish to a profound personal vocation.

5. Parish ministry for maturing adults shifts the focus of parish activity to a broad understanding of ministry at every level of mature adulthood: shared activities as well as shared growth in faith and life.

6. Parish ministry for maturing adults explicitly welcomes maturing adults into mainstream ministries of the parish.

7. The goal of parish ministry for maturing adults is spiritual transformation.

8. The content of programs offered in parish ministry for maturing adults rises out of the real situations in which such people live, including moments of transition and daily life.

9. Parish ministry for maturing adults focuses on both interior and exterior growth.

10. Parish ministry for maturing adults is Christ-centered.

11. Successful parish ministry for maturing adults is developmental, ongoing, and lifelong.

12. Successful parish ministry for maturing adults honors diversity of age, stage, personality, ethnicity, and spirituality.

Let's look now at each principle in some detail.

1. *Parish ministry for maturing adults pays attention to three dimensions of growth: spiritual, psychological, and physical.*

Maturing adults move closer to conversion and transformation when they can wholeheartedly embrace aging as a gift from God. Aging is part of the living water that God offered to the woman at the well, and by extension to all of us. Maturing adults become poised to achieve new levels of grace and peace heretofore unknown when they are equipped with the essential knowledge

> We need to invite and re-invite our maturing adults into the process of faith formation.

of how to mature. When fitted with such equipment, the aging process becomes an ongoing work of art, rather than a senseless slippage into nothingness, the first buds of the condition Pope John XXIII referred to as "youthfulness of spirit."

> When I think of my years…I sometimes feel the temptation to consider myself an old man. One must resist this; in spite of outward appearances, one must preserve a bright youthfulness of spirit. This pleases the Lord, is edifying to souls, and is good for us too, for it is our duty to infuse joy and optimism in others. Thanks be to God I prefer to look forward rather than backward. And I cherish the dearest memories of people and things in order to remind myself of the final reunion that awaits us. Life is rather like a long voyage. We set out waving and weeping as we part from our dear ones. But when we arrive the same people are already at the dock to await us. (Leone Algisi, *John XXIII*, pp. 161, 163)

The "youthfulness of spirit" of which Pope John XXIII speaks has little if anything to do with being young. Rather, it seems, and perhaps is, paradoxical that we must become very mature (wise) to achieve this youthfulness of spirit.

Much too often, spiritually maturing adults see the aging process simply as the secular world sees it: as something that happens to our bodies only. Aging is an extension of the God-ordained lifelong developmental process of life, and is therefore good. Aging is a spiritual process every bit as much as it is a physical and a mental process. In order to personally "own" this expanded view of aging, spiritually maturing adults need to transform any regressive attitudes about aging and replace them with life-giving attitudes of light. They need to be given life-expanding tools that equip them to deal positively and constructively with all that aging brings, the wonder and the diminishment. Here is the implicit challenge of parish ministry for maturing adults.

The average age of today's Catholic is rising; clearly, the average age of the people in the pews on Sundays is rising! Because of this, church leaders are often tempted to ask the question: How are we to sustain our mission and ministries with so few younger parishioners? Perhaps this is the wrong question. Perhaps a more salient question might be: How can we use and share the harvest of wisdom resident in our more senior parishioners to extend our mission and ministries? Such a shift moves us from a mentality of scarcity to a mentality of abundance.

At times it's relatively easy to see the advancing presence of God manifested in the lives of maturing parishioners. When we see clearly, we marvel at their spiritual stamina, humility, patience, acceptance, transcendence, simplicity, and so many other virtues. Grace like this powers a new transforming perspective on life that seems to reside in some elders so magnificently.

> We must define a new personal paradigm for aging that is built on a spiritual, rather than a secular, framework.

Such power can raise the overall level of wholeness in the entire parish, at least for those parishioners who can take the time to break through ageist barriers enough to appreciate the beams of grace shining from within our maturing adults. Perhaps this advantage is quite a sufficient reward for the parish as a whole. Yet, might there be ways of harnessing or tapping into the power of maturing parishioners in ways that can translate this power into new ministries, new apostolates, and new directions for service to the larger Church?

Our World Needs Wisdom

Our world needs more, not less, wisdom; indeed, our world craves wisdom. Our challenge is to find ways and means of connecting the innate wisdom of our healthy maturing adults with the needs of the world. With God's grace, we have to find new ways, new technologies of connection between the need for wisdom in our culture and the abundance of wisdom in our maturing parishioners. Chief among these new technologies of connection is, of course, the Internet.

As we mature we are ready to embrace spiritual development, to turn inward to claim the authority of our own wisdom as it is rendered in us by God. Spiritually maturing adults need guidance, as in every other stage of life, so they can become more aware of this.

2. *Parish ministry for maturing adults should be part of the parish plan, well organized, and consistent in offering services that people will come to count on.*

Anyone in your parish who works with older adults should be aware of the common misconceptions about maturation, but also about the fundamental emotional needs of spiritually maturing adults: reactions to loss, adjustments to aging, the need for spiritually helpful relationships, and the need for effective communication. Responding to these needs is at the heart and soul of their ministry and it is holy work.

Three bricklayers who were building a church were asked to describe what they were doing. The first said, "I'm laying bricks." The second said, "I'm building a church." The third said, "I'm helping to build heaven on earth." The third answer is a good one for parish ministers who work with older persons. Their goal is to help spiritually maturing adults gain increased insight into their own faith walk and to give them the precious gifts of heightened self-esteem, sharper independence, and wholesome understanding on a human level, so they can better practice and even celebrate their faith on a spiritual level.

Other goals include assisting them in achieving higher levels of functioning, maintaining a stable mood level, and slowing down the deterioration of functioning and wellbeing. Change is constantly taking place in their lives, and when we develop better insights into the way these changes are affecting them, we are better able to minister to their needs.

3. Parish ministry for maturing adults employs styles of teaching and learning unique to the people being served.

Spiritually maturing adults are best approached as adults, not as children. Pedagogy is the study of the learning and teaching principles necessary for teaching *children*. Since adults have different learning styles and needs, we need to approach them using "androgogy," the study of the principles and practices best suited for teaching *adults*. Androgogy rests on the principle that adults learn best when programs are designed to be personal, practical, and relevant. Adults can't help but learn when these three components are present in a learning situation.

Personal. Our programs cannot assume that all spiritually maturing adults have the same needs. Indeed, as we mature, we become more unique, not less so. Healthy maturation means that people steadily approach their own God-given authenticity, their own uniqueness. So we must not only allow for advancing individuality, but also foster an atmosphere and learning environment that encourages personality-specific learning and activities.

> "Spiritual development relates primarily to the person's willingness to respond openly to God, and an equal willingness to embrace the truth, at least as one knows it."
>
> —Benedict Groeschel, *Spiritual Passages*

Practical. Our ministry to maturing adults needs to have utility. Maturing adults ask: *How can this improve my life in a concrete way?* Theory is nice, but it's too removed from the everyday lives of spiritually maturing adults to sustain their interest. They are looking for great ideas, inspiring concepts, motivational insights, and global perspectives, but they want them in ways that make a down-to-earth difference right now.

Relevant. Relevancy speaks to how well the content fits into the maturing adult's spiritual life stage needs. A program about how to repair a furnace may be practical, but it's hardly relevant for the average senior adult's spiritual life.

4. Parish ministry for maturing adults is based on the idea that God is calling each maturing adult in the parish to a profound personal vocation.

Our efforts with maturing adults bear fruit when we recognize this and help them identify what their personal vocation might or could be and then help them sustain it through vocation discernment opportunities where they can look into themselves and discover their unique, God-given talents, and where they can develop plans for bringing these talents to full expression. All of us, including maturing adults, are happiest when our talents and gifts are being used in an environment of trust, encouragement, and affirmation. Paul enumerated an array of spiritual gifts in his letters to the Galatians, Philippians, and Ephesians. I have codified these into a spiritual gifts assessment instrument where spiritually maturing adults can discern their own gifts (see Appendix One).

Specialized vocations give new meaning to life. Many maturing adults feel a sense of meaninglessness because they've lost sight of their purpose. At every age and every stage we are continuously in the throes of deconstructing previous meaning systems and constructing new meaning systems in our innermost personality functions. Spiritually maturing adults need guidance, instruction, and dialogue with others on deeper spiritual levels so they can construct the most authentic and enriching life meaning possible. A fully vibrant ministry to maturing adults can remind them of who they really are, and hold up their inherent value in a new light.

In their wonderful little book, *Christian Adulthood: A Journey of Self-Discovery*, authors (and married couple) Evelyn and James Whitehead illuminate the importance of the parish in encouraging vocations development: "A faith community is not a neutral zone in which individuals pursue their separate vocations. Nor does a community provide vocations for individuals who would otherwise be directionless." They recommend that the faith community serve as the garden where the fruits of the Spirit are nur-

> Spiritually maturing adults need guidance, instruction, and dialogue to discern their ongoing spiritual vocation.

tured and given room to bloom into vocations, the seeds of which were planted by the Holy Spirit.

While the overall goal of our advancing spiritual growth and integration is to live daily with Christ, our maturing life vocation is perhaps best expressed in a more practical manner. Vocations that are specific, clear, well-defined, and focused seem most uplifting and even inspirational. Adults somehow feel more worthy, valuable, and useful when they can describe their vocation in a few simple words that are readily understandable.

I believe this can be facilitated thought the adage, "Work a day a week for Christ." Such a statement can become a theme of our parish ministry to maturing adults; it can accent the intentionality of our efforts and facilitate the evangelical quality of it. Older adults can then give testimony to their vocations and gain a heightened sense of meaning and the interior sense of well-being that comes from working for Christ.

5. *Parish ministry for maturing adults shifts the focus of parish activity to a broad understanding of ministry at every level of mature adulthood: shared activities as well as shared growth in faith and life.*

Most parishes have senior groups primarily for social, entertainment, and recreational purposes. The major "work" and yearly schedule of many such groups includes dinners, card parties, trips, games of chance, prizes, more trips, an occasional speaker (usually from a local funeral home, cemetery, or hospital), and of course, more trips. Notably absent from most senior group calendars would be social justice projects, spiritual reading discussion groups, any comprehensive faith formation events specific to their needs and concerns, or any participatory, liberating, or transformational learning. In short, there is no expectation of true interior growth. It's time for this to change. We desperately need to begin our journey beyond "senior group" thinking toward "maturing faith" thinking and practice.

Faith formation speaks to fullness of living, to integrating body, mind, and spirit, to the continual shaping and reshaping of personality, fostering growth ever closer to its true reality: the presence of God within. Faith formation is the process of passing the leadership of the total psycho-spiritual personality from our worldly self to our true and holy self. The faith formation process is not age or time-limited, rather it is driven by our very life course, our manifold life experience. It is the events, circumstances, relationships, travails, failures, successes, the full measure of our lives that offers us the spiritual curriculum we need to gradually let go of what is non-essential, and steadily turn toward the truth that sets us free. This is as true for older people as for everyone else in the parish.

6. *Parish ministry for maturing adults explicitly welcomes older adults into the mainstream ministries of the parish.*

Parish ministry is marked by hospitality, which means that we must be welcoming in all aspects of parish life and experience: social, physical, psychological, and spiritual. Our ministry to maturing adults is also marked by hospitality, which means that we must have social events where spiritually maturing adults are encouraged to mingle, mix, and have fun. But it also means that we must reach out to maturing adults who cannot come to church. It also means that we offer service and acts of compassion to assist maturing adults and create an environment of psychological safety and spiritual acceptance where issues of the heart and of personal meaning can find expression. Above all, it means that we invite and re-invite our maturing adults into the process of faith formation.

Getting such a process off the ground in the parish is not an easy task. Many maturing adults have had little preparation and even less background in faith formation. So we need persistence, determination, and an attitude that success comes over the long haul, not in "one-shot" programs casually listed in the parish bulletin. We need to invite and re-invite. The personal level is the only level that works with maturing adults. Remember, we must always be personal, practical, and relevant if we hope to succeed.

> Our role is to help maturing adults align their unique life experiences with the teachings of Jesus as they meet the unique mission of faith in their advancing years.

What needs to happen first, however, is a new way of thinking about the spiritual life. Spiritual growth is not something that stops at a certain point in our lives but rather is an ongoing reality that began with baptism and continues until we die. When Christ said, "I make all things new," he was speaking to all his followers at every age and stage about a continuous and ongoing process of spiritual growth. Older adults can continue to grow spiritually and many of them can also help others with spiritual growth.

CHAPTER FOUR

Guiding Principles: 7–12

In this chapter, we will continue our in-depth look at the twelve foundational principles for successful parish ministry to maturing adults.

7. *The goal of parish ministry for maturing adults is spiritual transformation.*

Moving to a mentality of abundance regarding the blessings of maturity in our Church first requires that we adopt new attitudes toward age and aging, attitudes best described as transforming. The prefix, *trans*, connotes "going over" or "going beyond." The root of the word, *form*, implies "substance" or "body." Adopting transforming attitudes about aging suggests that we grow beyond the level of "form" to a more ascendant level of perception and thinking. We advance when we can radically shift our beliefs about aging from ones involving loss to ones involving heightened opportunity for personal and spiritual development. Here is the heart of abundance thinking as opposed to scarcity thinking.

So often we become blinded by our own worldly attitudes that over-value personal achievement, production, and vocational performance above all other values. Too easily we equate *younger* with heightened performance and *older* with diminished performance. While such beliefs may dimly reflect reality on the form level, they clearly do not approach reality on a spiritual level.

Attitudinal transformation, with regard to maturing parishioners, requires change on two levels. The first level includes shifting our values, attitudes, and beliefs about aging itself, and about the very purpose of the Church, looking at our mission through a new lens. On the second level, we can think more creatively about new ministries for maturing parishioners, genuine ministries based on real human needs, not just simple tasks that have been elevated to ministry status.

Many maturing and even elder parishioners are repositories of knowledge, competency, and skill that have been tested by time and polished by experience. More than this, our mentally and spiritually healthy elder parishioners now glow with a new luster, a patina of grace that can be found nowhere else. How can this grace and glow, this wisdom of the decades be shared with others within and beyond the parish?

Here we need the nudging of the ever-present Holy Spirit within us to understand our own call to discipleship as well as to discern this call with our spiritually maturing adults. Perhaps our best response to the call of discipleship is in constructing a *true learning community* in our parishes, one that includes older adults. The kind of learning required for healthy spiritual aging is perhaps best defined as "transformative learning."

At its best, transformative learning equips the seeker of God to reflect upon her or his life experience and the shared life experience of other faith community

> As its name implies, transformative learning is about internal and personal change.

> Your only purpose today is to learn how to love better than yesterday!

members, and find the new life of Christ therein. Transformative learning enables seekers to see through the eyes of Christ and to change accordingly. This sometimes means to change one's very beliefs, one's way of viewing the world, one's way of making meaning of life, one's feelings and choices, and eventually one's actions. Indeed, transformative learning can be the vehicle we can best use in parish ministry for maturing adults to help them make all things new with Christ.

Transformative learning allows us to realign our true selves with God. Our true self sees the losses that aging brings not as threats or even as challenges to which we must adapt, but as instructive life changes helping us grow closer to God. We must take a more illuminated approach by seeing the changes of aging as part of God's eternal living water of love and as vanguards of our advancing maturation. With such a perspective, life is transformed from a senseless succession of losses into a generative curriculum for love and growth.

Perhaps the most personal, practical, and relevant task of all the senior years is creative change. Certainly, maturing adults are asked to change at a more dramatic rate and in more personally significant ways than in any other time in their lifespan. How can we seek this creative change in the full context of our Christian tradition? Francis Dorff, in his landmark book, *The Art of Passingover*, eloquently describes an entirely new way of viewing creative change in Christian terms. His work suggests that creative Christian living is a personal art form that we already know how to execute but which our culture and our personal fears may have caused us to bury deep within ourselves. Embracing change can be potent stimulation for personal growth and deeper spiritual understanding of the opportunities open to the spiritually awakening senior.

Judith Viorst's book *Necessary Losses* illustrates how we grow *because* of our losses, not in spite of them. We cannot become a toddler without losing our infancy, cannot become a child with leaving toddlerhood behind, cannot become an adolescent without leaving childhood behind, and cannot become an adult unless we pass through adolescence. Loss does seem to be a way we move through the stages and transitions of life. Life is a paradox; we have to lose in order to gain. But the gains are significant. What we gain is at the very heart of our reason for living. What we gain is an extension of the light that Christ brought to the world. We gain the opportunity to love better and deeper, more richly. We gain a deeper appreciation of the core of maturity, the center of joy, the piece of heaven within us. We gain in virtue development, love in action.

The life changes in the maturing years can be viewed as either a spiritual opportunity or as a threat. Continued growth and emerging happiness in the maturing years flows from the quest to discover new purpose, new meaning, and new life. If this cannot or does not occur, then spiritually maturing adults can become irritable, morose, and unhappy. Their spiritual and psychological growth and development are intertwined like no other time in their lives.

8. *The content of programs offered in parish ministry for maturing adults rises out of the real situations in which such people live, including moments of transition and daily life.*

One of the greatest transitions for older people, of course, is the dying process and death itself. Those who minister to them must acquire basic "how to" skills for helping those who are dying and their families. They must learn to appreciate the emotional stages experienced by the dying person as well as the emotional responses or stages that are likely to take place in those close to the dying person. It is important that they have an understanding of the process of bereavement and grief, that they know what behaviors to expect in the bereaved and the grieving—if they are to give real assistance.

Aging itself is another major transition. What does successful aging look like? Spiritually maturing adults of faith need a measure, a yardstick that gives them a clear picture of what constitutes health and wellness on all levels. The process of aging can be done well, or it can be done poorly. There are specific commonalities of successful aging; maturing adults and all staff and even volunteers need to know these as baseline or backdrop data. Such information can measurably increase their effectiveness since it provides them with a new definition of positive aging as a process that is God-ordained, the purpose of which is to learn better who we truly are in our heart and soul.

Incredibly, somewhere between three and four thousand Catholics retire everyday! With the average first retirement age in our country today at around fifty-eight, this means that many of these new retirees can expect to live another thirty years or more. What is our Church saying to these people who are entering a time of life identifiably different from any other that came before? What ceremonies, installations, or recognition does the Church give to the armies of its children as they begin this new life called "retirement"? What preparation for this new stage of living does the Church offer to retirees as the one institution that has consistently stood with them at every other stage of life?

How can the Church harness the power and energy in the

hearts and minds of its retired members? How can it offer opportunities for service, for works of care and compassion, peace and justice? How can the Church construct a vibrant ongoing formation curriculum that is unique to the stage and phase of retirement?

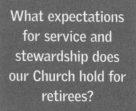

What expectations for service and stewardship does our Church hold for retirees?

Preparation for a comprehensive retirement cannot be accomplished with a calculator alone; many different factors enter the equation of success in retirement, chief among them spiritual development.

Retirement, like all of life, is primarily a new forum for ongoing spiritual development. Spiritually maturing adults have a need to define a personal path through the transition of retirement. They need to know that retirement isn't an end, but rather a new beginning; that retirement has a unique spirituality; that retirement is personally and spiritually growth enhancing; and that retirement offers a new balance to life that invigorates rather than diminishes.

It's surprising how many older adults, even those who practice their faith regularly, see no redeeming qualities to sickness. As a result, they develop a less-than-inspired attitude about the healing power of God. Spiritually maturing adults need to look at healing in a new way. The chronic ailments experienced by those in assisted and skilled care living facilities, for example, are difficult for many to accept. Maturing adults want to incorporate their faith perspective into their healing journey, but they just don't know how. They then adopt a purely "medical model" of relating to their sickness, seeing themselves simply as patients, rather than as fully authenticated children of God. Developing a new perspective on sickness makes all the difference in how spiritually maturing adults see themselves. This shift in perspective has the effect of positively affecting all parts of their personalities.

Wellness is an all-encompassing notion that includes finding fulfillment on three levels of mature human living. The first level of wellness is on the physical level; we simply call this "well." The second aspect of wellness is wellness of the mind, which we call "wisdom." The third aspect of wellness resides on the spiritual level of the soul, which we call "whole." At every life step and stage we seek to become well, wise, and whole. This is particularly important in the maturing years, for it's here that one has developed an adequate level of maturation necessary to really get a grip on these three aspects of wellness in a comprehensive way.

Spiritually maturing adults need a personal wellness program, a framework that gives them specific guidance on how to achieve wellness regardless of their objective health. Pursuing wellness and well-being in body, mind, and spirit is the foundational building block for personal development and positive change so necessary in the spiritually maturing adult years.

The entire Christian journey through life, purgation, illumination, and unity is a journey toward personal authenticity with God, a story of the unfolding of our true self, our self with God, our self in God. This journey is essentially a journey of wellness in its most global sense. God wants us to live life to the fullest at every stage of life. When we are living life to the fullest, we are living in *wholeness.* Wholeness means having a sense of integrity or becoming integrated. Wholeness is a condition of life where all our component parts are uni-

> Wellness is a state of being that emerges when and where one is functioning optimally at a physical, mental, emotional, and spiritual level.

fied into one harmonious unit. The opposite of wholeness is fragmentation.

One of the central competencies of a satisfying maturing lifestyle is the ability to connect at deep levels with one's spouse, friend, confidante, or mentor. Spiritually maturing adults need to be able to connect with others because it's in the midst of the relationships, in the words they say and the emotions they express, that they find their true self reflected. Maturing persons who have developed capacities and competencies for sharing themselves with others are some of the most emotionally healthy and happiest people. Sharing ourselves sustains us and allows our inner potential to take root and come to flower like nothing else can.

> We are called to focus on our spirituality, the hand of the Holy Spirit guiding us in the unfolding of God's action in our lives.

Every phase and stage of living demands change. Our lives are a continuous cycle of change. We are here to grow, to become all we can become. This process calls for change, change, and more change! Our choice is never whether we want to change; our choice is how we *will* change.

Parishes today are in the midst of a protracted process of change so profound that it has been called a "fundamental transformation." Forces such as ministry growth, shifting priorities, demands of an increasing aging membership, alternate residential styles, closing communities, as well as community and provincial amalgamation have exerted pressure on parishes that push and press for change. In this new paradigm, spiritually maturing adults are called upon to shoulder greater responsibilities for personal adaptation in an atmosphere of fluidity and consistent ambiguity.

For those maturing adults who have mastered the competencies of change, this new paradigm can be positive and growthful. For others, however, this shift can become stifling. They become emotionally over-burdened and begin to suffer what author Alvin Toffler dubbed "future shock" over thirty years ago!

9. Parish ministry for maturing adults focuses on both interior and exterior growth.

Maturation implies growth, a sense that the individual is moving in a positive and constructive way toward addressing the specific growth tasks of body, mind, and spirit. Unfortunately, growing older does not automatically imply maturity. With advancing maturation we are called to shift our perceptual focus more toward our interior life, the interior space where God resides within us. As we mature, we grow closer to that transcendent understanding of living in the world, while not being of the world. This paradox is only one of many that begin to connect and bind together the patches of our life into a wonderful quilt of many colors. This masterpiece quilt keeps us warm and secure in the wholeness of God. The passing years exact a toll on our physical frames, but they can add substantially to our spiritual stature, and, indeed, this is God's plan. Our developmental steps are but milestones of loving; our life course moving closer to God is a march powered and inspired by love that gives us life in abundance regardless of our age or physical condition. How can our Church connect God's love, the central belief of our Catholic faith, with the reality of aging in today's world?

In Dr. Jane Regan's keynote book *Toward an Adult Church*, she asserts that we must shift our primary focus of education in our parishes from children to adults. She claims the best way to do this is to concentrate on the needs and concerns of adults as the basis for sustained and sustaining adult faith formation. She makes a potent point that by focusing on adult needs and adult concerns, adults will discover new levels of interest in the parish. Not only will adults gain information for leading more healthy and wholesome lives, not only will they be better equipped to cross the many developmental bridges that maturation requires, but more than all these benefits combined, the chief benefit is in gaining a practical awareness of the presence and action of God in their lives and in the communal life of the parish. All these benefits apply to spiritually maturing adults as much as or even more than to younger ones.

The changes that later life brings can be received as opportunities or as threats. The purpose of later life is to usher in a renewal of spirit where a new forum for growth and happiness can emerge. This forum is inside us where the kingdom of God resides. Part of the personal work necessary is to bring one's interior world into sharper focus, finding a more comfortable balance between the outside and inside worlds. Growth and happiness flow from the quest to discover new purpose, new meanings, and new life.

10. Successful parish ministry for maturing adults is Christ-centered.

Our ministry to maturing adults needs to be a direct reflection of the mission of Jesus. Jesus came to bring us closer to God; we go to God through Jesus. Jesus' mission is a mission of education; he constantly taught, constantly proclaimed that he had come to bring a new order, a new and hopeful message that love is the strongest power in the universe. Successful parish ministry for maturing adults is an extension of this mission of love. Learning as personal transformation is at the heart of this ministry. True learning, learning from the Lord that is genuinely life changing, involves some measure of re-shaping of self.

Parish ministry for maturing adults needs to aim for the heart, offering new motivation, new understanding, new confidence, and new life. It helps people to imitate Christ—to perceive with the eyes of Christ, to think with the mind of Christ, to feel with the heart of Christ, to choose with the will of Christ, and to perform with the courage of Christ. This kind of faith is the way people find meaning in their lives.

For each of us at any particular point on our maturation journey, this is the first time we have come this way, the first time we've been asked to address this unique developmental task. This means that we are always amateurs in our developmental journey. We need mentors to help us along the way. All of the variables that go into our total faith experience provide the necessary backdrop for us to become the most authentic persons we can be in this time of life. Put more directly, our faith allows us maximal wellness at each stage of life.

Our Spiritual Story

The senior years are sometimes called "the wisdom years." In them we can unearth treasures of heart and mind, spirit and soul that have otherwise rested peacefully while awaiting discovery. "Wisdom making" requires that we flesh out and color the underlying script of our lives, always a spiritual script. As we do, we give our lives meaning far beyond what we could have otherwise deciphered; we find wisdom.

Our lives are punctuated by times when we seek a deeper understanding of the meaning implicit in them. As we move through our senior years, we wonder what we have really learned on the journey of life. This life learning is a central part of the overall developmental work of the later years. It is natural and normal to undertake what's been called a life review. Life review is the process that encourages us to pay close attention to the memory, to internally investigate it, turn it around in our minds, flesh it out, and make it more real. We try to discern the central theme of the story, our story. We try to determine what significance the innate theme of the story had for our life at the time when it was first lived. Finally, as we review it, we seek understanding of what it could mean in our life right now.

> Ongoing faith formation gives us the glue, the internal cohesion we need to live life in abundance. The glue is the light of Christ.

It is perhaps not until the budding wisdom of our senior years, when some internal urge motivates us, that we realize the unifying quality of our lives was there all along, but only vaguely and fleetingly recognized for what it was. It may not even be the mental image of the memory that catches us, but rather the feeling associated with the event that captures us. The feeling returns again and again until we are all but forced to deal with it.

A Spiritual Autobiography

Such a life review is vastly deepened when we take the time and reflection to enumerate the times when the Spirit of God rested upon us so gently yet firmly, directing our way and illuminating our path. Such a reverent life review is simply called a spiritual autobiography. Spiritually maturing adults can teach themselves to view the events of their lives as steps on their faith journey over their lifespan. We need to develop this unique perspective different from the day-to-day perspective we have used for so long. In our later years we have the luxury of viewing our lives differently; we can see that we are indeed living a unique adventure of our own making, that is, along with the Spirit of God. As we move farther along the lifespan, we gain both the personal history and the time necessary for a fuller discernment of the meaning of our lives.

> Our personal life story is an adventure that needs to be lifted up as a unique rendition of how God's love "works" in the world. It has all the components of a spiritual best seller: brokenness, confusion, redemption, forgiveness, transformation, enlightenment, tragedy, and peace. On and on the saga unveils the redemptive work of God. It is a love story of grand proportions. It's only in our senior years that we can capture these wondrous memories and weave them into an integrated tapestry. (R.P. Johnson, *All My Days*)

It is in midlife when the story of our true spiritual development into the senior years begins in earnest; it is in midlife when we set down the foundation of the rest of our life. In his book *Aging as a Spiritual Journey* (a true classic in the field), Eugene Bianchi spends more than half of his pages thoroughly describing the importance of the spiritual growth in the middle years as the preface for the accelerated spiritual growth in the later years. He states: "Unless the inner conversions of middle age take place, there is little hope that elder hood will advance beyond the growing despair and selfish concerns attached to gradual decline" (p. 8).

It's in midlife when, for the first time for most of us, the primary search in life turns inward toward a deeper relationship with God. Midlife ushers in a new profundity to life. Adults need the opportunity of looking deeply into their spiritual development in the middle years. Spiritually maturing adults need to look back to their midlife experiences as the advent of their present development. The middle years, generally thought of as between ages forty-five and sixty-five, are also filled with potential turmoil. Along with the inherent questions stirred up by one's confrontation with mortality, those in the middle years

> What came before our middle years was a prelude, a preparation for our fantastic journey of interior growth.

are "charged" with setting down the foundation of the second half of life. This is a process that takes the rest of life and which advances spiritual authenticity, our quest for God.

Spiritually maturing adults need ongoing spiritual development, and so too does any professional and non-professional staff that may be working with or even around older persons. The most personal, practical, and relevant spiritual care relates directly to the life experience of the person, i.e., what's happening in their lives right now because that becomes the "stuff" or content of their ongoing spiritual development. Middle-aged folks need to confront their own mortality, they need to mourn the loss of their youth, they need to tolerate contradiction in their lives, and they need to identify and articulate their preferences, among other spiritual developmental tasks of midlife. By successfully addressing these and other age-appropriate developmental tasks, staff and volunteers can enhance the effectiveness and the satisfaction of their work.

11. Successful parish ministry for maturing adults is developmental, ongoing, and lifelong.

There is never a time in a Christian life when the person can claim, "Well, I guess I've grown spiritually as much as I can." Our lives are divided into stages that are hooked together by transitions. Noted developmentalist researcher Daniel Levinson calls them the "seasons" of life. Whatever name we give them and whatever chronological demarcations we ascribe to them, we do move from one life stage to another. No life stage is more important than any other, each has its place, and each has its own learning. We call the learning in each stage the "tasks" of that stage. Generally, we need to perform tasks to move from one stage to another. For example, on that wonderful day when we first learned to walk upright on our own two feet, we moved from the late-infancy stage to the toddler stage. Each stage and phase has its own life tasks, its own learning that we are called to undertake and accomplish. This notion applies not only to our physical and psychological tasks, but also to our spiritual tasks of life as well. There are certain spiritual developmental tasks for midlife, for example, others for the Boomer stage of development, still others for the Builder stage, and even others for the Elder years. No time on life is spiritually empty; no time in life can be wasted.

Humans are experiential beings, not existential beings like angels. As such we are bound to grow. We either grow or we begin to die. We cannot not grow; we cannot stand still, we cannot mark time, we cannot simply "hold on." Either we are moving forward or we are moving backward. Each of us grows in our own unique way with the framework of the specific work of that life stage. Our unique, holy self lies within us; our job in life is to set that unique, holy self free as much as we can. Just as a sculptor chips away at the virgin stone removing from it all that is unnecessary, debriding the stone as it were, of all that hides or hinders the true and authentic form emerging from

> The true and authentic self gradually surfaces from beneath the confines of the barren human ego.

it, so too we and the Holy Spirit form an artistic team charged with our spiritual development. God gives us the raw materials, so to speak, and the grace (power) to accomplish the task, but we must pick up the mallet and chisel and start actually letting the masterpiece of who we authentically are emerge from the barren and virgin stone.

Sometimes we make only timid and tentative strikes with our mallet, and our authentic self emerges from within the stone only very slowly. At other times we act boldly, striking the mallet with passion. At these times, huge chunks suddenly drop from the stone. The encumbering shroud of stone, the ego self, falls to the floor and is reduced to debris to be swept away, revealing the masterpiece God intends us to be, more free than ever before. Here is a metaphor for conversion in the senior years, how the stone is transformed from a block of stone into an inspirational masterpiece, engendering awe and inherently reflecting the beauty of God.

We must actively participate in our spiritual growth; it doesn't happen by itself. We've been given free will; we can choose to participate at whatever level in the conversion process we want. But, participate in the process we must. Our active volition is a requirement for spiritual growth. When we accept the Holy Eucharist, how passionately and lovingly are we doing that? If we are nonchalant in our acceptance, casual in our intention and thought, then the value of the Eucharist will likewise be devalued for us. Is that the fault of the Holy Eucharist? Of course not. Our lack of love, our lack of intensity and involvement with Christ blocks the full measure of conversion from finding its home in us.

If and when we fail to actively participate in our ongoing spiritual growth, we suffer consequences beyond stunted growth; we experience pain of one sort or another. What do we lose when we fail to actively participate in God's redemptive plan for us, when we fail to involve ourselves fully in conversion? It would be easy to say that we simply suffer from a retarded spiritual growth. Yet, is that all? Might we also suffer other "consequences of the spirit" that might not be readily apparent to us as we move through the routines of our lives? Consider the spiritual pain of non-involvement, of submissiveness, living a lackluster life of stagnation; we become emotionally crusted, shallow, two-dimensional, and cognitively concrete. Other consequences of lapsed spiritual growth might include feeling useless, washed-up, having no purpose in life. Finally, we can experience the pain of existential floundering, having no direction, nothing real to stir us, motivate us, drive us, enlighten us. Our life lacks awe, wonder, and delight.

Spiritual growth is, to some degree, intertwined with all other human growth: physical, emotional, and psychological. We are holistic beings; one level of growth cannot dramatically outpace the others if we expect to be balanced and integrated. We need body, mind, and spirit. We seek integration, all the various parts of us operating in alignment, in coordination. We seek to become a unified *bodymindspirit* single entity, rather than three separate ones. Toward that end, spiritually maturing adults seek to be as well in body as they possibly can; they invest their time and energy in keeping their bodies functioning as smoothly as possible, regardless of any physical diagnoses they may be dealing with.

Likewise, spiritually maturing adults seek intellectual stimulation, they seek to be as emotionally and psychologically balanced as possible, they wish for themselves the most uplifting attitudes, most clear and accurate perspectives, and the most forward thinking possible. Finally, spiritually maturing adults seek spiritual insight, spiritual experience, growth in virtue development, and a closer communion with God.

> Conversion is the radical transformation of the self during its ongoing development.

Spiritual growth occurs in an orderly sequence. Conversion is our goal in life; conversion is necessary for us if we are to continue our forward movement along our road to salvation. Our conversion speed accelerates in our later years; our level of cooperation with the Holy Spirit's gentle nudging determines the speed and depth of our conversion. All spiritual developmental tasks are steps we take with the Holy Spirit; each brings us closer to our unique authenticity, the real self within us. As we progress in our way toward God, to become more like God, to more clearly manifest God in our modern world, we gradually chip away at the excess and the unnecessary in our lives.

Happiness comes from appropriately addressing the various work or tasks of our life. What does it mean to be happy? In its most basic and richest sense, happiness emerges in us when we take the opportunities to express our unique gifts, the ones that God has invested in us quite intentionally and uniquely. Our job is to reflect God's love, to light a corner of darkness. We reflect God's love through expressing our giftedness. We find happiness to the extent that we accomplish this reflection, even in the smallest ways. Love flows through us, but when we become indifferent to this flow, when we neglect it, rather than trying to actively foster the flow, we lose our grip on true happiness. It's at this point that we seek substitutes; as the country-western song suggests, we are "looking for love in all the wrong places."

12. Successful parish ministry for maturing adults honors diversity of age, stage, personality, ethnicity, and spirituality.

The first tenet of adult development is that as we mature we become more different from all other people. God seems to like diversity and evidently wishes that the uniqueness that God has injected quite intentionally in each of us becomes as fully expressed and behaviorally realized as possible (consider the parable of the talents). This spiritual developmental process toward personal authenticity, the fullest flowering of one's infused spiritual giftedness, is the implicit goal of all faith formation efforts.

We may find the first compelling reason for adopting a vital parish ministry for maturing adults when we take a developmental perspective on maturation, especially spiritual maturation. The church is most healthy when it offers diversity. Age diversity is perhaps the most universally recognized diversity in most churches. All the various age groups in the church are intertwined. The ability of one cohort of people in a church to successfully meet the developmental challenges of one stage provides the needed communal context for other cohort of persons to successfully address their proper and appropriate developmental tasks as well. We are not in isolated developmental boxes; we are all in the same pot. When one ingredient doesn't or can't express its unique flavor, then the others cannot express themselves fully either. One part or element of the parish or faith organization system affects and is affected by every other part; it's like family systems theory.

Maturing adults are not one homogenous group. Instead, the larger group is best divided into several cohorts or age groups. Such sub-groups, or cohorts, can be seen as addressing similar developmental tasks; they are in relatively the same growth stage of life. For our purposes, we refer to three divisions of the larger group: Boomers, Builders, and Elders (see page 9).

Research into "thinking styles" curiously tells us that as we mature we move away from relying on a strict rational and linear thinking style consistent with left-brain thinking, and move toward the more intuitive and associative style of thinking associated with right-brain thinking. I've noticed that healthy adults advance to ever increasing spiritual enrichment and interest, not less, as they mature. Perhaps this is what Paul meant when he said, "we walk by faith (right-brain), not by sight (left-brain)."

Loss is a common visitor in the lives of spiritually maturing adults, loss that can be irrevocable. Loss is a fact of living on this earth. Many spiritually maturing adults who are not blessed by a strong faith may condemn loss as a process that shouldn't be happening; they take every means to insulate or otherwise protect themselves from it. On the other hand, spiritually healthy adults often bless loss as a means for richer spiritual depth.

The later years present losses unlike those encountered previously. How we adjust to these losses or diminishments creates the story of our later life development. Some spiritually maturing adults enter their later years with personalities that have suffered under a progressively cascading insufficiency of personality development. They have encountered anemic or even regressive personality growth over the years and hence are truly

> Emotionally and psychologically healthy maturing adults live rich, affective, and intuitive lives.

impaired in their abilities to adjust to their later years. We call such persons chronic problem or difficult personalities.

Among all the various personalities, five have been identified as chronic problem or difficult personalities in the later years. These are: depressed, anxious, dependent, delusional, and angry. Often, older persons who experience emotional difficulties are dismissed as "cranky," "just getting old," or even "senile." When labeled in this manner, appropriate ministerial and pastoral care becomes stilted and forced. Spiritually maturing adults involved in parish ministry for maturing adults need to understand the characteristics of older adults with emotional difficulties and the reasons for their sometimes baffling behaviors. Spiritually maturing adults in parish ministry for maturing adults, and especially those who are in leadership or service positions, staff and volunteers alike, need to know some practical caregiving skills for managing these difficult persons. Equipped with such understanding and skills, they can provide sensitive care and companionship that will enrich the lives of the older persons God sends to us to serve and from whom we learn.

Spiritually maturing adult Catholics involved in their parish parish ministry for maturing adults can become more aware of these various difficult personalities so they can interact with them in the most healthy and loving ways. Persons, even the most caring and gracious persons, who are not aware of such personalities, can unwittingly slide into interaction patterns that might best be described as toxic. When this happens frequently, the whole effort of parish ministry for maturing adults is jeopardized.

CHAPTER FIVE

A Model Organization

Naturally, there are many ways that an individual parish can address the spiritual needs of its maturing adults. There are, however, some commonalities that can serve as a blueprint. I see the organization and construction of a vibrant parish ministry for maturing adults as progressing along these seven steps:

1. Identify a leader

2. Construct a team

3. Leadership training and motivation

4. Census and needs assessment

5. Spiritual education programs

6. Outreach and service programs

7. Motivation, follow-through, and evaluation

Step 1. Identify a Leader

Every successful parish ministry to maturing adults (and any other program for that matter) needs a person who is in charge, a person whose responsibility is to serve as the catalytic agent, primary visionary, and energy source for the program. In short, we need a director. Certainly, it's common for a parish to have a youth minister, an individual appropriately educated and equipped to organize, lead, and shepherd a vibrant program for the young people in the parish. I see the ministry of parish ministry for maturing adults as a similarly important position in the parish; it requires an individual who is educated and equipped to shepherd a vibrant program for maturing adults.

What are the qualities of a leader in parish ministry for maturing adults? To answer this I turn to work that Sr. Mary Corde Lenn, OP, and I accomplished some time ago. We were interested in the intangible notion of "spiritual luster." Spiritual luster "sits" on three overarching personal qualities: being a light of Christ, demonstrating the beauty of Christ, and expressing one's spiritual distinctiveness. It struck me that the findings of our research around the construct of spiritual luster would be a productive platform for describing the general personal characteristics of an effective parish minister for maturing adults. These characteristics are arranged in rank order from highest to lowest:

Prayerful: the ability and practice of being with the Lord and pondering the sacred.

Faith driven: an overriding value that one's life is motivated by one's committed beliefs.

Real: the quality of being true, genuine, and authentic with self and others.

Radiator of Christ's peace: the knowledge of and ability to project the serenity of the deep peace of Christ.

Committed: the ability to steadfastly focus on a goal and sustain personal engagement toward its completion.

Balanced: a personal quality in which the whole of one's life operates in harmony.

Affirming of self and others: the ability to empower and motivate action in oneself and in others toward a selected goal.

Listener: the sensitive ability to respond to the needs of others.

Respectful: the ability to honor others and allow them to be themselves.

Optimistic: the ability to witness and spread joy.

Tolerant: the ability to accept, operate in, and even thrill in the holy contradiction and sacred paradoxes of life.

Responsible: being accountable.

Principled: being counted on as honorable.

Adaptable: being flexible and personally supple.

Relational: having the ability to communicate on both content and affective levels so as to generate human bonding.

Humorous: the ability to react to and touch life lightly.

To be successful, a parish minister for maturing adults (director) doesn't need to have an advanced degree in gerontology; she or he doesn't need an MBA, or an extensive resume of experience in management. What the director does need is a vision and a commitment. The director needs an over-arching perspective of the goals and objectives of a comprehensive parish ministry for maturing adults and a sense of personal mission and purpose to point a direction, chart a course, and remain steadily on track. Many colleges and universities offer gerontological programs, even advanced graduate degrees, yet these programs tend to be much too theoretical and academically cumbersome for the needs of a parish. Most of these programs are geared for students who will eventually address the medical, social, or basic care needs of elders such as transportation, meals programs, legal or work counseling, housing, and the like.

Such academic programs are all to the good, yet, without more personal, practical, and relevant training, they can miss the mark for persons interested in focusing on the spiritual developmental needs of maturing adults. A different sort of education is needed for those wishing to make a spiritual difference. They don't need graduate degrees to become effective in parish ministry for maturing adults, yet they do need practical training, solid and practical attitudes, skills, and competencies that provide the foundation to bring the parish ministry for maturing adults program to excellence. The director needs to know how to integrate spiritual growth with knowledge of the maturation process. He or she needs to be supported by practical resources and needs the tools, skills, and knowledge base to truly make a difference in the lives of the maturing adults. (See Chapter Seven's section on mini-courses, which describes components of the kind of education the director requires.)

Step 2. Construct a Team

The director cannot function alone and needs to be supported by a team. This team can be called the leadership team, the support team, or the parish ministry for maturing adults council. As a group, the team has many general responsibilities, including

- consulting with and giving counsel to the director,
- animating the vision of parish ministry for maturing adults,
- serving as the representative body of parish ministry for maturing adults to the parish,
- "talking-up" parish ministry for maturing adults,

- encouraging others to become part of parish ministry for maturing adults,
- reviewing and evaluating possible programs for the parish ministry for maturing adults,
- evaluating the needs of maturing adults in the parish,
- identifying potential key or talented persons,
- communicating with the pastor and parishioners, and
- collaborating with the diocese, other parishes, and churches in the community.

In addition to the general responsibilities of the team, each member of the team, or subsets of the team, can also assume specific responsibilities or tasks that foster smooth and efficient operation. Suggested committees on the team might include:

Education and spiritual growth: responsible for identifying suitable programs that enhance the spiritual development of maturing adults.

*Person powe*r: responsible for recruiting and organizing volunteers.

Program development: responsible for keeping all programs moving forward.

Funds development: responsible for raising whatever money is required to keep the parish ministry for maturing adults enterprise running well.

Social: responsible for the communal aspects of the ministry.

Community outreach: initiates, organizes, and serves as leadership for all outreach programs.

Step 3. Leadership Training and Motivation

The first order of business for the director and the leadership team is to become as well informed about parish ministry for maturing adults as possible. This book is a good first step. The team should also consider going on a retreat as a means of spiritual grounding and inner life motivation. This second step should not be rushed. In our eagerness to "get things going" we sometimes give only scant attention to training. Team training and team building is essential—it equips each team member with facts, attitudes, perspectives, and goals absolutely essential for effective ministry to maturing adults. Beyond that, training motivates and inspires team members; it galvanizes commitment and builds *esprit de corps* in the team. There is no replacement for good training.

Co-Workers in the Vineyard of the Lord, a statement of the United States Conference of Catholic Bishops, gives an extensive and excellent overview of the components of the formation process for lay ecclesial ministry personnel. The bishops point out that there are four general areas of formation:

Human formation: basic emotional and psychological health.

Spiritual formation: "aims to arouse and animate true hunger for holiness, desire for union with the Father through Christ in the Spirit" (page 38).

Intellectual formation: "seeks to develop understanding and appreciation of the Catholic faith, which is rooted in God's revelation and embodied in the living tradition of the Church" (page 42).

Pastoral formation: "cultivates knowledge, attitudes, and skills that directly pertain to effective functioning" (page 47).

I refer you to this publication for an in-depth overview of these four general areas of formation. The wisdom presented in a condensed form there can give guidance to the director and members of the leadership team.

Step 4. Census and Needs Assessment

The director and leadership team need census data about the population of Boomers, Builders, and Elders in the parish. They need to know the demographics of the three populations, including age, the percentage of this group represented in the entire parish population, etc. The second large area of interest is a spiritual gifts assessment of all spiritually maturing adults. In Appendix One you'll find a Spiritual Gifts Survey for Maturing Adults that you can copy and use for this purpose. Once this data is collected, the leadership team needs to study the dispersion of spiritual gifts in the three populations and determine how these gifts can best be put to use.

A note of caution: whenever one collects data from any one individual or group, the surveyor has the obligation to convey the results of the survey to that person or that population. This requirement can be an effective means of spreading the word about parish ministry for maturing adults throughout the parish. Once the results of the survey have been tabulated and studied, the director and leadership team can communicate these results in several ways. They can compress the results into a parish document, publicize a summary of the general results in the parish bulletin, or call a meeting of all who were surveyed to review the results. This event can also serve as a convenient time and place to further outline the vision and goals of the parish ministry to maturing adults.

Do not send out a survey to all older adults in the parish asking what they want in a new ministry program. *Do not do this!* What you will get back is some

> "Those who go are those who follow; this is the paradox of faith. Those who teach are those who have themselves been taught."
>
> —Keith R. Anderson and Randy D. Reese, *Spiritual Mentoring*

variation of "buses, bingo, and brownies," i.e., a list of diversionary and socializing ideas. While play and companionship are certainly important components of any ministry for maturing adults, they do not constitute faith formation. Jesus directed us to "Feed my sheep." Buses, bingo, and brownies (and especially trips to the local casino) do not feed sheep! I know that this seems undemocratic and perhaps even a bit arrogant but the answers you get might take you in a direction you don't want to go, certainly not as your primary focus. There are two types of programs that every ministry for maturing adults ministry *should* have: spiritual education programs and outreach programs. In my experience, a synergistic blend of these two creates the most vibrant ministry for maturing adults.

Step 5. Spiritual Education Programs

In this step the team makes the call as to what spiritual educational program(s) can be most productive for ministry to the maturing adults in the parish. In Chapter Seven, you will find content and rationale for various courses or programs of study that I recommend. Naturally, these programs are best introduced one or two at a time. When you finish the sequence you have chosen, it will be time to start offering them over again. (For information about faith formation options for maturing adults, consult the website www.senioradultministry.com)

Step 6. Outreach and Service Programs

Besides educational programs, a healthy ministry for maturing adults needs to offer outreach and service programs. There is no lack of problems in our society, and no lack of talent among the spiritually maturing adults that God has placed in our parishes. How do we get these two together? One way is to affiliate with already existing programs. Such affiliation can be with existing diocesan programs or with ecumenical social service organizations in your area.

Helping others can be a stimulating spiritual endeavor for your older parishioners. And not only do outreach programs stimulate individuals, they motivate and galvanize your entire ministry around an identifiable purpose that is clearly visible. This needs to be seen as a vocation, not simply volunteer activities. Pursuing a vocation gives each maturing adult a message of new life at a time when it's needed most. Outreach service programs are the natural "action" extension of all the spiritual developmental interior work that you encourage in your educational programs.

Here is a list of possible service programs that your ministry for maturing adults can either sponsor or undertake on its own:

Friendly visitor
Handyman
Meals-on-Wheels
Transportation
Peer counseling
Mentor programs
Retirement Readiness Outreach
Coffee Shop Ministry
Homeless shelters and services
Services for abused children, spouses, and families
Affiliation with diocesan programs
Elder issues and services
Housing needs
Addictions education programs
Wellness discussion and support group

Healing circles
Growing Ageless in the Lord's Eyes study group
Finding personal meaning in the third age group
Adult children education and support group
Faith life review and autobiography group
Bereavement group
Senior Bible studies
Fundraising
Social activities and travel
Habitat for Humanity
Child care services
And many, many more!

Step 7. Motivation, Follow-Through, and Evaluation

Quality spiritual education and targeted outreach programs are motivational in and of themselves. However, both leaders and spiritually maturing adults require inspirational motivation and encouragement to keep the flame of the Spirit alive. Plans need to be realized, they need to be put into action, and for this to happen you need follow-through. Efforts, sometimes on a Herculean scale, need to be devoted to bring plans off the drawing board and into the hearts and hands of the people involved. Ministry to maturing adults is really an effort of re-evangelizing right within your own parish. Evaluation, of course, is very important and it is an ongoing process. Each and every program, step, decision, and new direction needs evaluation.

CHAPTER SIX

Ministry Components

No two ministry programs for maturing adults are alike. They may subscribe to the same guiding principles and adopt similar organizational structures, but the specific programs they offer and outreach efforts they support may look quite different. Here are some components you might want to consider for your own ministry.

Monthly and Weekly Meetings

In addition to ongoing educational gatherings and outreach projects, the entire parish ministry for maturing adults membership should meet at least monthly for a dinner and some sort of program at the church. Such programs can include speakers from the community or older parishioners themselves who have a special message. Only one criterion is absolutely necessary: the theme of the program must be directly or indirectly related to ongoing spiritual development. Monthly meetings are most successful when they are sub-group oriented, i.e., Boomers and Builders generally hold separate monthly meetings. The most successful meetings are a mix of community life, planning for the future, affirmations for group and/or individual accomplishments, new information, and prayer.

Spiritual and Sacramental Growth

Prayer is central to any ministry for maturing adults. It is essential for both personal and organizational growth. Prayer binds us, heals us, fosters forgiveness, deepens peace of mind, promotes a sense of well-being, and most of all, gets us in-touch with our true selves. Every gathering is better when it begins and ends with prayer. Rosary recitation, healing prayer, intercessory prayer, prayers of thanksgiving, mourning, praise, celebration—all are appropriate for gatherings with maturing adults.

Monthly Day of Prayer and Recollection

Days of recollection that include Scripture readings, time for individual meditation and contemplation, and opportunities for personal reflection and faith sharing strengthen our faith formation efforts with maturing adults. Hosting such a day each month will greatly animate your overall program. The best results come when the day is scheduled at the same time each month, for example, the second Tuesday, or the third Thursday. It can begin at 9:30 AM and end around 3:30 PM.

The format can be flexible, perhaps opening with a Scripture reading followed by group prayer and quiet reflection. This can be followed by a presentation about spiritual development. (Chapter Seven's curriculum list can be very helpful for the topic selection process.) You might also want to include small group discussion of thought-provoking questions. Dividing the larger group into subgroups keep the day lively and interesting. A shared lunch offers time for community building and socialization. The day might end with a summary statement on the theme and a special blessing ceremony led by the pastor.

A Look at the Future

Sybil, director of ministry for maturing adults at St. Elsewhere Parish, reviews her schedule for the month. First, she checks off the weekly meeting of the leadership team. Next, Sybil reviews the programs for the month. Mondays and Thursdays are reserved for ongoing educational programs. The first Monday is reserved for classes on basic competencies of parish ministry for maturing adults. The second Monday is a class on retirement preparation and retirement living as a spiritual journey. The third Monday is training for caregivers; the fourth is health and wellness training. The four Thursday classes deal with knowledge about faithful aging, healing and health promotion, personal spiritual development, and spiritual conversion and transformation training.

When a cycle is completed, Sybil schedules a month of Bible study. (See special section in Appendix Three, References for suggested Catholic Bible study programs). After a month of Bible study, change is needed, so she follows up with a second round of Monday and Thursday classes. Monday classes include bereavement studies, spiritual companion, mentor/coach training, spiritual gifts and talents discernment, and forgiveness training. The second round of Thursday classes are dedicated to leisure identification and applications, spiritual personality review, healing sessions, group spiritual direction, spiritual gerontology, and developing a deeper understanding of self.

This second round is again followed by a month of Bible study, after which a third round of classes is offered. This time the topics come from the participants themselves; they also serve as the instructors. Course content and descrip-

> Prayer transforms the group beyond itself and onto a transcendent level.

tions vary widely. These may include computer training, golf, needlework, singing, genealogy, journal writing, play reading and production, book discussion groups, etc. There is no end to the topics that emerge from energized people.

Support Groups

Here is where Sybil wants to expand the offerings. Currently, she administers several support groups. On the first Tuesday of the month she facilitates an "Adult of Aging Parent" support group. This gives caregivers an opportunity for learning, sharing, and identifying with others in similar situations. This sharing relieves needs, soothes hurts and emotional pains, and provides respite from the sometimes grinding routine that caregiving can bring. On the second Tuesday, a trained volunteer coordinates a "Faith Life review" group where participants write their spiritual autobiographies. The third Tuesday is the ongoing bereavement support group, and the fourth Tuesday is always wellness improvement. Over the years, other support groups have formed, run their course, and, when interest waned, they closed. All this is to be expected, and demonstrates the vitality of ministry to maturing adults.

> If aging is our master teacher, what is it teaching us? That as we age we need more virtue development, more love in action, more mercy, and more compassion.

Certainly your own parish ministry to maturing adults cannot begin with such robust offerings. Start small, perhaps beginning with the Monthly Day of Prayer and Recollection. Once this has taken root, introduce one educational class and one Bible study. Follow this with service projects and a social event.

CHAPTER SEVEN

Addressing Ongoing Spiritual Needs

This chapter itemizes and describes the specific content areas that offer a rich and comprehensive curricular base upon which you can construct an effective parish ministry for maturing adults. For the past twenty years I've searched for information, ideas, insights, attitudes, concepts, and feelings that can best equip maturing adults to meet the challenges that a spiritually expanding later life can bring. This chapter outlines the fruit of my search, arranged and described in a way that can best position maturing adults to find Christ in their everyday lives.

There is only one way your parish ministry for maturing adults can capture the excitement and vitality of God's plan for middle and later-life spiritual development, and that is by constructing a true learning community. There is an emerging body of knowledge I call "spiritual gerontology and maturing adult development" that can serve as the underpinning for a curriculum. Keep your maturing adults learning and you will be successful!

> The best ongoing spiritual development is built on life experience.

Ongoing spiritual development for adults in their maturing and the elder years needs to be purposeful, organized, intentional, and developmental. Too often we find spiritual development efforts offered in a manner that seems to lack direction, structure, and an integrative framework. In many parishes, ongoing development for spiritually maturing adults is little more than hit-or-miss offerings that satisfies no one—not church leadership, not the coordinator, and certainly not the spiritually maturing adults themselves.

Working with spiritually maturing adults is a special calling. This special calling or vocation needs continual and consistent encouragement and reinforcement. All the people who work with spiritually maturing adults, in whatever capacity, need help in redefining and realigning their personal vocation with the mission of the Church. Ongoing spiritual development brings us closer to God, closer to our true selves, i.e., God within us. It is best practiced as a sequence of educational experiences that generate deeper and deeper insights about our true nature and our relationship with God. These experiences flow quite naturally from our God-ordained developmental path, those life stages and transitions that make up our total life experience.

Personal Spiritual Development Inventories

Personal spiritual development inventories represent the next step in parish ministry for maturing adults and are a constructive addition to your overall ministry to older parishioners. They give an accurate reading of each person's spiritual development in current time, are easy to take, and the results are truly motivational, even inspirational. You can jump-start your ministry to maturing adults with such inventories. (See www.senioradultministry.com for a complete list and full description of all the Spiritual Development Inventories I have used.)

Spiritual assessment is still in its infancy stage in our Church, but the movement is growing very fast. All of us want to grow spiritually, but how do we know if we are progressing well? Each stage and phase of life has its own spiritual lessons to teach, but how do we know if we're on track? This is the job of the inventories, to offer a firmer grip on one's own spiritual development, a clearer understanding of where we are spiritually, and thereby help us gain new insight and motivation into those areas of spiritual growth that might be most beneficial for us now.

Measuring spiritual development may at first seem strange or even unnecessary. Isn't spiritual growth something that's between me and God? Isn't my spiritual development a matter of conscience, not some quantitative measure comparing me to some unknown norm group? Spiritual growth is indeed a personal communion that resides in the relationship we nurture with God on a strictly personal level. Yet, there are commonalities in the overall thrust of spiritual development and faith formation, especially with maturing adults. We now have the technology to identify where an individual stands in relation to an established scope and sequence of spiritual development in general. Such efforts offer a panoramic insight into our progression in our spiritual development journey.

> All of us are charged with growing toward God and in so doing becoming more and more the persons we truly are.

Over time we gain the necessary strength and understanding of how to surrender the direction of our life to God. This ongoing faith development is called the process of authenticity, becoming who we truly are in God's eyes. Authenticity is something we seek all the days of our life. Personal spiritual development inventories give us the unique opportunity to "get a fix" on our progress and help us make whatever modifications might be suggested in the inventory.

Mini-Courses for Maturing Adults

Each of the mini-courses outlined here contain information that together constitute a comprehensive educational program for maturing adults. The courses are flexible in that each can be given in a short or an extended time frame. They can be offered in a variety of settings and formats that include formal classroom instruction, retreats, workshops, one-on-one mentoring, and a discussion-group format.

The courses can be given (and taken) in any sequence. Most described in this chapter can be offered to Boomers, Builders, and Elders groups. I would caution you, however, with something I learned long ago: don't mix Boomers, Builders, and Elders in the same course! This is unfortunate, but true; it is based on an inbred fear of aging. Boomers do not want to be seen as "old" or even aging; consequently, they will boycott programs they view as geared to "older" people. I suggest that you avoid the words "older," "aging," and the like in your course titles and descriptions.

You will be most successful when you target your offerings to one group or another, but not all three at the same

> Christ transforms the journey of the later years from a pointless succession of diminishments to an adventure in soul expansion.

time. You might even want to give different titles to essentially the same material that can be "shaped" especially for the Boomer, Builder, or Elder populations. For example, Mini-course #3, like most of the courses, works very well with Boomers, Builders, and Elders. However, you might find a few Builders coming into a Boomer class, but you generally won't find Boomers going into a Builder class. Such age segregation is not unprofessional; it's simply good marketing based on experience. There may be times when you will bring all groups together, but these times will not be for content-based programs; rather, these times would be for intergenerational mixing or healthy competition.

Each of the courses described on the next few pages are brief outlines of full courses offered by the JOHNSON Institute, www.senioradultministry.com.

12 Basic Competencies

Audience Parish ministers who work with maturing adults

Purpose To offer basic skills and attitudes for understanding and working with maturing adults

Content Beyond having a willing heart and a giving hand, persons interested in working with spiritually maturing adults (as well as older adults themselves) need to learn these basic, essential competencies.

1. Envision parish ministry for maturing adults as character development with spiritual depth. Personal authenticity and spiritual truth are the overall goals of all parish ministry for maturing adults efforts.

2. Recognize and overcome ageist barriers. Misconceptions about aging abound in our culture and by extension, in our Church. Ageism needs to be countered in our parishes because it can keep our older parishioners from living fully as they seek the abundant promised by Christ. Ageism also diminishes self esteem.

3. Use factual data and accurate adult development concepts. It is important that maturing adults become well acquainted with the facts if they are to correct their own attitudes where needed and counter ageism when they detect it in others. Most importantly, with a greater fund of knowledge about aging, we will be better equipped to make positive contributions enhancing the dignity and respect of spiritually maturing adults.

4. Understand and respond to the actual needs. Spiritually maturing adults, no less than younger ones, experience a

multitude of needs. We can sometimes forget that beyond their basic needs, spiritually maturing adults also have other special needs: medical attention, income, status, personal security, personal grooming, as well as the need for recreation, transportation, and socialization.

5. Recognize the fundamental requirement of building and maintaining effective caregiving relationships. A helpful relationship builds up each person in both personal and spiritual ways. The major goal is to enable Christ to enter the relationship, to allow the healing power of God to permeate it. The central core of the relationship is the spiritual development of both the maturing adult and the caregiver.

6. Adopt attitudes of facilitative helping toward spiritually maturing adults. As a seedling needs air, water, and light to be nourished and grow, a relationship requires certain necessary conditions for its maximum growth.

7. Facilitate positive and meaningful attitudes among spiritually maturing adults. Maturing adults can learn to what degree they are aging successfully, and they can be equipped to give direct and effective help to others so they can sustain a positive and meaningful attitude about themselves. This is a core ingredient of successful aging in faith.

8. Use basic communication skills. Anyone who works with spiritually maturing adults needs to master some of the basic communication skills that are central to any effective helping relationship. Good communication skills determine perhaps more than anything else just how successful the ministry to maturing adults will be in a parish.

9. Understand and exercise communication techniques that identify and clarify emotional feelings. Three positive communication skills are

1. searching for meaning,
2. focusing on feelings, and
3. Making feelings-meaning responses.

Each of these fosters deeper and more helpful sharing on the part of the spiritually maturing adult and will serve to activate parish ministry for maturing adults efforts on any level. Try to avoid the three "un-skills":

1. giving unsolicited advice,
2. offering personal analysis and interpretation, and
3. giving false reassurance.

10. Utilize specific communication skills that help spiritually maturing adults gain increased self-understanding and enhanced behavioral direction in their lives. True and genuine care of spiritually maturing adults first takes faith; it then involves our conscientious and heart-felt support, a support that requires the ability to communicate positively.

11. Foster a faith-filled life review with spiritually maturing adults. Life review should be looked upon as a natural and potentially uplifting, spiritually enhancing process, as an experience that is practiced, to a greater or lesser degree, by virtually all spiritually maturing adults. The process may vary in intensity among spiritually maturing adults and differ in the ways it is experienced, but it appears to be universal in spiritually maturing adults.

12. Deal confidently with death and dying, as well as bereavement and grief. Death, of course, is part of life; without death life would seem hollow, almost senseless,

yet we resist it. We are confronted with a death or dying situation and we see a tragedy. Even when death slowly descends upon an older spiritually maturing adult, eighty-five and older, our emotions are still stirred, our feelings are moved, we can become shaken temporarily, and we can lose our effectiveness. Maturing adults can come to better understand death in a very personal way and to clarify our own attitudes and values that can either burden us or give enhanced meaning to life.

The 12 "Keys" of Successful Aging

Audience   Maturing adults

Purpose   To offer basic information and encouragement
about how to age well

Content   This program emerged from my research around
a singular question: What factors, forces, and personality traits allow a person to mature (age) well?
To my surprise, as the four-year study unfolded, it
became apparent that I was uncovering what I've
come to embrace as a central fact of positive
aging: we age best when we invite God into the
process. Our advancing faith is the golden thread
that runs through all positive aging. These twelve
"keys" emerged as the fabric of that golden thread,
the solid core of how to age well.

1. Transform our attitudes about aging. Aging is as much an
emotional, psychological, and spiritual process as it is a physical one. When this fact is fully recognized and embraced as
the primary understanding of aging, then the spiritually
maturing adult is ready to use her/his own aging as a catapult
for deepened personal and spiritual growth.

2. Seek love everywhere. Adults mature best when they sin-
cerely seek the presence of God in all they perceive and position themselves to realize a fuller potential of the love-power
that God has invested in them. When we cannot find love in
our daily lives, we become fearful instead of surrounded by
the love of Jesus.

3. Delight in connectedness. We find the light of Christ most clearly reflected in the eyes of God's children, regardless of their age. When we are in a genuine sharing mode with others we discover anew the noblest aspects of ourselves. Connecting in as full a way as possible is our true heart's desire and delight.

4. Live in the now. When we live in the past we find ourselves blinded and perhaps paralyzed with shame and guilt. When we live in the future, we find threat and fear as our companions. Living in the now gives us the delight and the joy to live fully and completely, for it is there we find the peace and strength of God.

5. Accept your true self. The virtue of acceptance is true spiritual "grit." Acceptance means embracing the truth, beauty, and goodness that God has placed in us. Acceptance of our true selves means we touch the divine in our hearts, walk the holy ground of the true reality of Jesus incarnate in the world.

6. Forgive others and yourself. Forgiveness is the bridge we walk over to discover happiness. Jesus taught us about forgiveness, and when we enter into the gentle flows of forgiveness grace running through us, we touch the gentle healing of God within. Forgiveness is the ultimate unburdening. Spiritually maturing adults need the balm of forgiveness to break out of the bonds of guilt that may have bound them to pain and isolation for far too long.

7. Let go of anger and other inner turmoil. Anger is a mature human emotion as long as it doesn't hurt anyone and doesn't fester into a grudge. Some older adults, especially those who have incompletely addressed the spiritual and psychological developmental tasks of midlife, enter their later years holding a cache of anger that thwarts their ongoing spiritual growth.

8. Give yourself to others. Altruism, giving of oneself without expecting anything in return, bequeaths many gifts: a sense of euphoria, staving off depression, feeling more comfortable, and even decreasing aches and pains.

9. Celebrate your faith. Much research is surfacing now showing proof that persons who practice their faith are generally healthier. These benefits are enhanced when persons go beyond the external practice of faith and embrace the more interior aspects of faith.

10. Discover personal meaning in life. Living a meaningful life seems tied to spiritual development in more than a simple and casual way. True meaning comes from associating one's life course and personal activities with an overarching coherence. This coherence, or sense of personal integration, emerges from living a Christ-centered life.

11. Make your feelings work for you. Spiritually maturing adults experience as much emotional breadth and depth as do younger persons. This rich, affective world motivates action that may seem hidden because it isn't manifested in external, achievement-oriented ways; rather, feelings in later life are more prone to stimulate the interior action of attitudinal change.

12. Achieve balance in life. So much of successful living in later life is built on a strong, and more importantly, a balanced life structure. Spiritually maturing adults adjust to the many losses inherent in later life by investing their energy more or less equally among the six life arenas of work, family, relationships, self-esteem and body image, leisure, and spirit.

MINI-COURSE #3

How to Find Peace and Purpose

Audience   Parishioners who are preparing to retire

Purpose   To offer basic skills and attitudes for making retirement spiritually meaningful

Content   Each retiree and potential retiree has much to consider; each must look into himself or herself with a keen introspection, a view that has probably not been used for many years, if ever. This self-inventory is crucial if a new and fulfilling retirement lifestyle is to emerge. Failure to undertake such a personal assessment leaves one at great risk of descending into the grip of living a lackluster or distracted retirement lifestyle where the mission and ministry of Jesus Christ is only a peripheral part. Here are the retirement success factors that my research indicates need to be analyzed if the pre- or post-retirement Catholic hopes to find the true joy of Jesus Christ.

Career reorientation: Successful retirees need to psychologically move away from their full-time job as their primary source for self-identity, and emotionally, psychologically, and spiritually take on other activities that support a self-esteem of new definition.

Retirement value: Catholic retirees need to give worth and significance to retirement as a personally meaningful time of life. Retirement is not an end, but a new beginning; retirement is an entirely new spiritual development movement destined to transform every facet of the individual's life.

Retirement is not personal fragmentation, desolation, and purposelessness. Retirement is life enrichment, healthy self-ownership, and creative self-reliance.

Personal empowerment: Catholic retirees need to rely on their own internal sense of self-direction for making plans and decisions for their retirement life, rather than relinquishing their volition to the cultural media, the fads of the time, or the societal directives about what a successful retirement should be.

Physical wellness: Catholic retirees need to pursue wellness on all levels: physical, mental, and spiritual. Wellness is an overarching concept that allows us not only to look and feel our best, but more importantly, serves as a vital backdrop for retirees allowing them to express their God-given gifts to the Church and to the world.

Monetary adequacy: Catholic retirees need to financially plan well for their retirement years. Adequate monetary support gives sufficient security so the retiree can address the full scope of his/her life with creativity and purpose. Want of the necessities of life blocks one's full measure of action and curtails one's ability to live abundantly as Jesus promised.

Present happiness: Noted author and Jesuit Fr. John Powell wrote a book entitled *Happiness Is an Inside Job*. We create our own happiness, and, if we've been successful at creating happiness for ourselves before retirement, chances are very good that we will continue to do so after retirement.

Future happiness: Retirees need hope for the future. We all need to believe that tomorrow will be a time of personal fulfillment and joy. If we cannot achieve this sense, we suffer the tragedy of losing hope.

Spirituality and life meaning: Retirees need to feel they are living a life of meaning. The only way we can experience such meaningfulness is to pursue a purpose, a dream, a life cause, a burning desire of a positive and constructive nature. We need to be committed to something bigger than ourselves.

Respect for leisure: Leisure has three purposes: rejuvenation for the body, stimulation for the mind, and enrichment for the soul. Leisure pays some uncommon dividends when we approach it from a spiritual standpoint. Leisure allows us to offer ourselves to others, to appreciate the beauty of God's domain, and to become grateful for all that God has given us.

Personal flexibility: Every measure of mental wellness includes our ability to be flexible, adaptable, and/or malleable. Retirement invites and even demands change in every arena of our lives. If we can't change, we don't grow.

Spiritual luster: Every retiree needs to experience the glow of the light of Christ. We are people of the light; Christ came to be the light of the world and has implanted that light in us. We are called to let our light shine. When we do, we find the happiness and peace that surpasses all understanding.

Caregiving responsibilities: Our life in Christ calls us to care for others; certainly it calls us to care for our family. With increased longevity, retirees are finding that they are enlisted into the ranks of caregiving more and more. Caring for aging parents and caring for adult children, along with caring for a sick spouse, can consume an otherwise placid retirement.

Home life: "Home is where the heart is." All others things being equal, a happy home life produces a happy retirement experience. Yet, the shock of retirement can sometimes create great turmoil in even the best homes. Without proper preparation, relationships at home can be stressed and strained to a breaking point.

Maturation vitality: Retirees need to see their very maturation process (aging) as a time of emotional and spiritual vitality and vibrancy, full of potential for dynamic and ongoing personal growth. Negative attitudes about aging or fear of aging, however unconscious they may be, place an unnecessary burden on the retiree.

Stewardship and service: Retirees can replace in retirement what they formerly received as benefits from their work. Beyond money, retirees need to replace other vital things as well. Among these life-vital benefits are socialization, time management, a sense of purpose, and a certain status. Retirees can replace these best by helping others through stewardship and service.

MINI-COURSE #4

Spiritual Companionship

Audience Parish ministers who work with maturing adults

Purpose To offer basic skills and attitudes for understanding how to be spiritual companions to older parishioners

Content What is a spiritual companion, and what are the skills, competencies, and knowledge that this persons needs to master? All who deal with maturing adults in a parish can become a spiritual companion. (The undergirding structure of this section comes from *Competencies for Gerontological Counseling* by Jane Myers and Valerie Schwiebert, a book I regard as the authoritative and definitive resource outlining the specific skills and knowledge required for effective counseling with maturing adults.)

Demonstrates positive and empowering attitudes about maturing adults and the maturation process in general. Aging needs to be seen as a normal part of the adult life cycle. As spiritual companions, we strive for a particular awareness that older adults are not fundamentally different from other adults. We yearn to develop attitudes that are empowering rather than patronizing, respectful in the fullest sense rather than discounting, and enriching rather than dispiriting.

Integrates lifelong faith development with normal human development across the lifespan. There are numerous theories of adult maturation; each attempts to explain how people mature and how they respond to their maturation process. The question of what is "normal" maturation is cumbersome at best. Yet, several theories have emerged that give us guidance for better understanding how Boomers, Builders, and Elders grow most healthfully into and through the various stages of maturation.

Has knowledge of social and cultural issues that impact maturing adults, especially as they relate to family functioning. One of the most pressing social issues for maturing adults is health care. The majority of persons over the age of sixty-five have at least one chronic aliment, chief among these hypertension and arthritis. Spiritual companions can learn about health care policies and have a general knowledge of the common health concerns of maturing adults. A second cultural issue is the pervasive arena of caregiving. More than eighty-five percent of all care given to mature adults comes from the family. Spiritual companions can gain a working knowledge of family dynamics and functioning, as well as knowledge of adult-child caregiving issues, each of which has direct bearing on faith developmental factors.

Establishes and maintains a faith-based facilitative relationship with spiritually maturing adults. Building quality relationships is essential for spiritual companions because a relationship is the fundamental forum within which human growth and spiritual development arises. Seven communication skills are vital for successful personal faith facilitation with maturing adults:

1. active listening,
2. attending to feelings,
3. valuing both the message and message sender,
4. allowing the maturing adult to speak for himself or herself,

5. creating an atmosphere of emotional safety,

6. encouraging maturing adults to talk about personally meaningful matters, and

7. providing constructive feedback.

Is able to assemble and maintain various kinds of groups with maturing adults, including prayer groups, spiritual autobiography groups, life review groups, etc. Groups are powerful health-giving mechanisms. Every parish needs to provide opportunities for maturing adults to congregate in groups settings. On a social level alone, groups provide interaction that combats loneliness and isolation, as well as stimulates the forces of life within us. Group participation is a vitalizing force which enriches a sense of belonging and offers satisfaction to our basic need for connectedness.

Enhances overall life meaning by integrating dimensions of faith into life transitions such as retirement, bereavement, sickness, and aging. Life transitions provide the essential backdrop for ongoing faith development. Transitions always involve loss and renewal. Transitions reflect one of the fundamental tenants of our faith, the centrality of transformation, conversion, and redemption.

Has knowledge of faith development assessment procedures and instruments. It may seem strange for assessment to be part of the job of faith formation companions; yet on an individual level, certain personal assessment instruments can be the best way of helping maturing adults find faith direction that they otherwise could not. Assessment instruments results give rise to personal insight and stimulate introspection, discussion, and life change. (See Appendix One for a comprehensive overview of spiritual assessment instruments.)

Is aware of the common personality distortions that can become burdensome to maturing adults and those who deal with them, and how these distortions can interfere with normal social and faith development. Our personality is our repository of all of our attitudes, perceptions, thoughts, feelings, decisions, and eventual actions. Even though our personality is considered stable, there are two forces that can contort it over time: any physical changes that affect our brain and a deterioration of our mental health due to lack of growth.

Is sensitive to the interconnections of body, mind, and spirit dimensions of human functioning, and has developed skills and knowledge which can assist maturing adults to thrive and not merely survive. We are body, mind, and spirit all bound up together, one affecting the other in ways both direct and mysterious. Spiritual companions who are aware of these interactions and interconnections, and who have learned competencies on how to address these, can better serve the full faith development needs of maturing adults.

Knows when it is necessary to seek further help for a maturing person beyond what he or she can provide, and knows places and people from whom the maturing persons can seek broader assistance. Many times the losses and changes maturing adults encounter require assistance well beyond what can be appropriately addressed by the spiritual companion, so they need to have a rudimentary knowledge of available resources in the community.

MINI-COURSE #5

A Faith-based Perspective of Sickness

Audience   Caregivers, maturing adults, and all who work with maturing adults

Purpose   To offer basic guidance for dealing with sickness from a faith perspective

Content   Sickness doesn't need to be debilitating, certainly not from a spiritual perspective. Over eighty-six percent of persons over sixty-five years of age have at least one chronic ailment. Personal impairment comes more from the way that spiritually maturing adults see their illness, than from the illness itself.

The example of the woman with the hemorrhage (Mark 5:21–34). For twelve years the woman with the hemorrhage had suffered; she had spent all her money on physicians and she was now desperate. She heard Jesus was coming through her village and was intent on simply touching the hem of his garment. What was the force that motivated her? What internal strength possessed her to take the action she did? This holy impulse changed her life dramatically.

Searching for God's healing power. Each of us, and perhaps spiritually maturing adults even more so, is reaching for the hem of Jesus' garment, in our way seeking healing for all sorts of brokenness in our lives. We pray, we wish, and we wonder how we can move closer to God and find the healing power that we desire. We live in a material world where physical forces are always at work. Things break, mistakes happen, and yes, tragedy strikes. Still we search for those connections between our sickness and the healing power of God that we know is there for us if we only knew how to best access it.

Diminishment is part of life. In our later years especially, we experience events of diminishment happening all around us. During these times we are called, more than ever, to reach out for the hem of Jesus' garment. These diminishments or losses, which include losses in every arena of our lives, challenge us to our very core. Such losses invade our personality and cause a cataclysmic cascade of change that sends threatening shudders of vulnerability rippling through us. Spiritually maturing adults need to develop a new frame of reference about their sickness and all maladies of diminishment that may befall them.

Sickness vs. illness. The words "sickness" and "illness" are often misunderstood. Sickness refers to a condition of the body when some part (or parts) of it may somehow be broken or malfunctioning. Illness, on the other hand, is entirely distinct from, yet connected to sickness. Illness refers to our emotional, personal, psychological, or spiritual reaction to our sickness. It's very possible to be very sick but not ill. Sickness simply happens to us, while we, directly or indirectly, volitionally or not, create our own illness. Doctors try to cure sickness; the Church's domain is healing illness.

Physicians treat, but only God heals. Our faith is our central strength, and we, like the woman with hemorrhage, seek to reach out for the hem of Jesus' garment. God is with us always; our job is to listen deeply, always trying to understand what healing path God intends for us. We can sometimes get in trouble when our own egos attempt to dictate to God rather than deeply listening to God's voice inside us. We alone try to outline what healing path, what material outcome would be the right one; we try to tell God what God should do. It's easy enough to say, "Let go and let God," but it's probably the hardest thing we are ever called to do.

MINI-COURSE #6

A Holy Understanding of Wellness

Audience   Maturing adults, caregivers, parish ministers to maturing adults

Purpose   To offer basic information about the meaning of wellness

Content   Wellness means iving fully. Full living means finding maximum fulfillment from all areas of life: occupational, familial, financial, relational, educational, spiritual, and physical. The definition of wellness that I like the best for maturing adults is "having a chronic sickness and taking very good care of it." Eighty-six percent of persons beyond the age of sixty-five have at least one chronic sickness. Wellness has clear attitudinal qualities and is not simply the absence of disease. Health is a very personal thing; a state of thriving, not simply surviving. This concept becomes even more focused with the adage, "Wellness means adding life to your years, not simply years to your life!"

Four Goals for Wellness

1. **Building lifelong wellness:** doing what is necessary to keep the marvelous machine of one's body in top running condition.

2. **Mastering the psychology of leisure:** developing and maintaining a mindset that values the ideas, events, activities, and relationships that foster leisure.

3. **Taking charge of life:** striving to shoulder dependable and responsible action so growth and development occurs smoothly in the various arenas of life.

4. **Energizing the positive:** seeing oneself on a continuous self-improvement program and regularly striving to make oneself better today than yesterday.

The Art of Living Wisely

The second thrust of total wellness and wellbeing is becoming wise. The term "mental wellness" probably comes closet to being wise. Being wise doesn't mean that a spiritually maturing adult has amassed mountains of wisdom. Rather, it means that the person has developed methods of approaching life that allow her or him to think clearly, accurately, and rationally about self and others.

Characteristics of living wisely

Maximizing personal resources. The "wise" generally make decisions on their own rather than being unduly influenced by outside forces.

Creating healthy relationships. Perhaps because of their internal confidence, spiritually maturing adults who pursue a wise life enjoy people.

Learning the art of exceptional living. Wise adults proactively seek to inject change into their lives. They look forward to change to make things better.

Actualizing wise expectations. They view all the events in their lives, even the ones that may seem offensive on the surface, as further opportunities for personal growth and development.

Pathways to wholeness or personal integration. When persons are whole, they have personal integrity and all the pieces of their life are cohesively held together by unifying principles. This integration or wholeness allows them to live with an overriding sense of peace this world cannot give. The four characteristics of those who practice wholeness are

1. **Finding natural peace and harmony.** Spiritually maturing adults pursuing wholeness give their energy to all the arenas of their life.

2. **Harnessing the power of purpose.** "Whole" maturing adults derive meaning from their lives because they have a life purpose, a goal that is bigger than themselves.

3. **Living in the now.** Wholeness includes developing the means and skills necessary to keep morale high.

4. **Honoring the real self.** They view their life experiences as life advantages rather than as weights pulling them down.

MINI-COURSE #7

Caregiving as a Forum for Spiritual Growth

Audience   Caregivers of maturing adults

Purpose   To offer basic information about ways caregiving leads to deeper spirituality

Schedule   This course can be offered at any time of year using the following formats: over three successive weeks, two hours each; on two successive Saturdays, two hours each; over the course of a single week (shared among several parishes)

Content   In the fourth commandment, God calls children to honor their parents. Likewise, God calls spouses to love "till death do us part." Indeed, we are all called to care for our sisters and brothers, but especially children and elders. When caregiving is elevated to the spiritual level, when it is seen through the eyes of God, then it becomes a new forum for personal development, a new arena for spiritual growth, and a new launch pad for heightened inspiration. How then can this shift from the material, physical plane to the spiritual plane be accomplished? How can we learn to see caregiving in the new light of God?

The classroom of caregiving. Caregiving offers lessons in the classroom called life unlike any other efforts we can take. Where but through caregiving could caregivers learn the true meaning of faith, hope, charity, kindness, and mercy? Indeed, we can only come to learn these lessons when we actually experience their opposite, and the turmoil of caregiving usually provides us with an ample amount of the opposite, paradoxically in the midst of loving care. How magnificent is this learning model that teaches us how to love better today than we did yesterday.

Needs of caregivers. The very first need of caregivers is information. Catholic caregivers require information so they can give the best care possible without endangering their own health, well-being, or spiritual growth. This information falls into six categories.

- Caregivers can develop an understanding of the needs of their cared for and their own as well. This understanding includes a deep sensitivity to emotional needs as well as the more easily recognized physical needs.

- Caregivers must come to recognize the role of loss in the lives of older persons as well as their common emotional reactions to loss.

- Caregivers can learn to develop and strengthen truly healthy relationships with the one for whom they care. Such a relationship is the fundamental element of caregiving. It includes the three conditions of any quality relationship: genuineness, warmth, and unconditional positive regard. These mirror the love and acceptance of God.

- Caregivers can learn how to break down barriers that may exist between themselves and the care partner. Examining attitudes about aging and older persons in general is useful for the caregiver, as well as recognizing how myths about aging may be playing a role in one's caregiving.

- Caregivers can foster positive communication between themselves and their care partner.

- Caregivers can learn active listening and psychological attending skills; listening to the meaning behind words and offering empathetic feedback. Communicating empathy requires skills to reflect content and feelings.

Sharing the love and the redeeming message of Christ helps caregivers maintain positive and meaningful attitudes. Knowing factors that contribute to "successful aging" and incorporating the notions of life stages and transitions into one's thinking are useful for both caregiver and their care partner.

Come to a profound understanding that the final end of caregiving is not "fixing," but rather the end of mortal life. Knowing the five stages associated with death—denial, anger, bargaining, depression, and acceptance—helps caregivers deal with death and grief. A hospice can provide support if and when the need arises.

The Dynamics of Personality in Later Life

Audience Maturing adults, their caregivers, and all who minister to maturing adults

Purpose To offer basic information about personality change and development

Content As we mature, our personalities continue to develop. However, ten to fifteen percent of maturing adults descend into any one of the five behavior patterns described in this course. Such persons can be difficult to deal with; they may resist help, frustrate those helping them, and can even be obnoxious at times. It's important for us to monitor our own reactions to such difficult behaviors. It's easy to become angry or frustrated. These reactions can lead to avoidance of the difficult person and, in extreme cases, can lead to compassion fatigue. There are healthy ways of dealing with such personalities, ways that allow us to transcend their behavior and deal with them in a more Christ-like manner.

Negative Behavior Patterns

The *angry* older person expresses anger that is only rarely connected with the present; generally the anger is deep-seated and pervasive. Angry persons can become suspicious and see others as rejecting, certainly not as concerned and caring. Some common reactions to this behavior include defensive of one's own actions, nervous in the face of anger, fearful that something awful will happen, apologetic and placating, and/or angry right back at the angry person. None of these reactions to the angry person is productive. We need a better way.

The *dependent* older person expresses an urgent quality to all her/his requests. They have difficulty making independent decisions, they seek an unusual amount of advice, and they like to rely on the judgment of others. Such persons believe (unconsciously) that they are inadequate or incompetent. Perhaps the most difficult thing for others to understand is the fact that dependent older persons have expectations of limitless help and assistance from everyone around them.

The *depressed* older persons can exhibit many different behaviors and attitudes, the most common are general unhappiness, pessimism, irritability, feelings of inadequacy, lethargy, and low self-esteem. They often experience sleep difficulties, have poor self-care behaviors (but not always), and can complain of many different physical symptoms. They are generally indecisive, unfocused in some ways, pre-occupied, and uninterested in social interaction.

The *anxious* older person can exhibit a variety of mood states, including feelings of dread and impending doom, excessive worry, fear (generally without a known reason), and vague feelings of uneasiness, to name but a few. They generally exhibit or experience many different physical sensations such as tightness in the chest or throat, unstable GI tract, shortness of breath, insomnia, dizziness, frequent urge to urinate, rapid heart rate, sweaty palms, and appetite disturbances.

The *delusional* older person can exhibit behaviors that are seen as bizarre at times. A delusion is something that is accepted as truth when it is actually false or unreal. Delusions are common in skilled care facilities where older persons are confined and may begin to lose their sensory bearings.

MINI-COURSE #9

10 Spiritual Developmental Tasks
of the Middle Years

Audience   Boomers, parish ministers to maturing adults

Purpose   To offer insights about spiritual development

Content   Our spiritual development requires our active and continuous participation. There is never a stage of life when we can stop our involvement in our ongoing spiritual growth. Just as we need to eat daily to ensure our physical survival, likewise we must take active steps every day to ensure our ongoing spiritual growth and development.

Finding Personal Integration

The following ten spiritual developmental tasks of midlife are posited as dialectics, as opposing conditions. Our job in midlife is to find personal integration between each of them. Eventually, one side gains dominance over the other, not by conquering it or by pushing it out of the way, but rather by draining its energy and incorporating this energy into the opposite side of the dialectic. The tension that is generated by the struggle with each side is the forum for our spiritual growth; it is from this tension that our growth emerges. Without the struggle, we do not grow.

1. Looking Ahead vs. Looking Behind: the degree to which we can start measuring our life in terms of time remaining rather than measuring life in terms of time elapsed.

2. Living Youthfully vs. Living as a Youth: the degree to which we can let go of the things of youth and take on the maturity of having to work for our own youthfulness.

3. Assimilating Contradictions vs. Demanding Consistency: the degree to which we can begin to understand the role of paradox in our lives and the fact that personal contradictions exist within us, as opposed to rejecting these and demanding that all things and persons remain forever sure, constant, and fixed.

4. Evolving an "Other" Focus vs. Remaining "Self" Focus: the degree to which we can shift our primary concern from an egoistic viewpoint to one that places the needs and desires of others as of at least equal importance to our own.

5. Reconstitution vs. Fragmentation: the degree to which we can reconcile with our own brokenness and the brokenness of the world and embark upon personal renewal.

6. Consolation vs. Desolation: the degree to which we can shift our view of God from a God who "makes all things right, right now," to a personal, loving, and healing God.

7. Purposeful Living vs. Purposelessness: the degree to which we can discover or re-discover our personal dream, our individual mission and pursue it with passion.

8. Positive Change vs. Fixation: the degree to which we can reorganize our personality by injecting constructive and spiritual modifications into it.

9. Life Enrichment vs. Idle Busyness: the degree to which we can gradually shift our definition of self away from simply being a producer and achiever, and more toward a self-definition of "being" on the inside.

10. Self-Possession vs. Self-Forfeiture: the degree to which we can more fully "own" our true selves, taking it back from whatever factors and forces that may have hampered our innate freedom in the past.

MINI-COURSE #10

Developmental Tasks of the Builder and Elder Years

Audience   Maturing adults, Builders, Elders, those who minister to them

Purpose   To offer basic information about spiritual development for Builders and Elders

Content   The Builder and Elder stages are times of graced and gracious growth. As the body slowly diminishes and shows the signs of the physical disintegration due to the aging process, the heart and soul more fully integrate. It's been said that with age, one's body slows down while one's spiritual pace quickens. Spiritual development in the Builder and Elder stages can propel spiritually maturing adults to new and exciting heights of heart, mind, and soul.

Ten Dialectical Tasks

The following ten spiritual developmental tasks of the Builder and Elder years are posited here as dialectics, as opposing conditions through which we find personal integration. As in previous stages, we seek personal integration, harmony, and peace by finding a synthesis between the powers on each side of the dialectic. One side eventually gains dominance over the other, but generally not before we enter the struggle. The tension that is generated by the struggle between each side of the dialectic is the forum for our spiritual growth; it is from this tension that our growth emerges.

1. Transformation vs. Powerlessness: the degree to which we become more personally empowered by the message of the eight beatitudes.

2. Living Mystery vs. Self-Reliance: the degree to which we allow ourselves to walk more by faith and less by sight.

3. Dealing with Physical Diminishment vs. Denying Reality: the degree to which we can more clearly see the discomfort and suffering caused by our bodily changes as invitations for spiritual deepening.

4. Confronting Self vs. Self-Absorbed: the degree to which we can plumb the depths of our authentic self and discover there our spiritual uniqueness.

5. Mentorship vs. Becoming a Critic: the degree to which we find and exploit avenues for passing on whatever wisdom we may have learned.

6. Becoming Involved vs. Falling into Alienation: the degree to which we have found ways of exercising good stewardship of our time and talents.

7. Wisdom vs. Confusion: the degree to which we have developed a spiritual understanding of life that gives a unifying order to our soul.

8. Innocence vs. Irritability: the degree to which we can rediscover our child-like qualities of awe, wonder, and delight.

9. Taking Stock vs. Dependency: the degree to which we can arrive at the profound spiritual truth that God's hand has been upon us at every step of our life journey.

10. Creative Completion vs. Fear: the degree to which we can face death creatively, with forethought, insight, and spiritual anticipation.

MINI-COURSE #11

The Dynamic Spiritual Power in Relationships

Audience   Maturing adults

Purpose   To offer basic information and encouragement about relationships

Content   What makes for a quality intimate relationship? Whether the level of that intimacy is very close, as in a marriage relationship, or whether it is a very close friendship, the notion of intimacy is still operative. My professional experience, research study, and clinical observation, together with all the mistakes, failures, and even the successes I've had in my own relationship, have taught me that there are six essential qualities that successful close relationships of all types must practice on a continual basis.

Most people learn them only through an ongoing process of interaction, negotiation, perhaps some turmoil, and of course, lots of patience.

Relationship Eroders and Relationship Evaporators. Relationship eroders wear away at the six relationship essentials, eventually wasting them away. A chart of the six relationship essentials, the six eroders, and the six corresponding evaporators, can be found on the next page.

The job of any partner in an intimate relationship, whether this is a friendship, mentorship, or some other relationship where personal connection is desired, is to stay in the center, in the relationship essentials, as much as possible, and help your friend, partner, significant other, etc., do the same without dominating, manipulating, or otherwise imposing.

Evaporators	Essentials	Eroders
Disengagement	Togetherness	Self-centeredness
Pedestrianizing	Respect	Resentment
Appeasement	Communication	Criticism
Possessiveness	Intimacy	Defensiveness
Blind Faith	Trust	Doubt/Insecurity
Co-Dependency	Commitment	Indifference

Connecting with God. A relationship rises to its spiritual peak when partners stay as centered as possible in both their six personality gifts, and in the six relationship essentials. When the six relationship essentials emerge ever more potent, stable, and sure in a relationship, *and* when each partner's personality gifts are encouraged to grow and express themselves freely, lovingly, and cleanly, it is then that the relationship enters new territory and moves onto holy ground, a sacred space. As this emerges, the relationship as a unit develops a revered triadic connection between God and each of the partners.

The six spiritual conditions that will grow in any intimate relationship as you use your personality gifts and the six relationship essentials are

- sacred unity
- spiritual faithfulness
- transcendent prayerfulness
- holy groundedness

- redeeming forgiveness
- blessed uniqueness.

These six are impossible to achieve by ourselves alone; they are only possible with God's help. They are fostered when the relationship partners open themselves to God's infinite healing power. Our God-given personality gifts are that infinite healing power working within us.

MINI-COURSE #12

On Becoming a Mentor

Audience Maturing adults, ministers to maturing adults

Purpose To offer basic information about mentoring for mature adults

Content A mentor is an ordinary person of faith who has made the conscious, intentional decision to help other people of faith who would like to discover a clearer vision of Christ in themselves and translate this vision into a personal, practical, and relevant retirement life vocation. Mentors help maturing adults get a firmer grip on what God's plan might be for their maturing years.

Finding Personal Meaning. Certainly, maturing life offers a different pace of living, but just like every stage and phase of life, our true heart's desire is to love and be loved. We can love and be loved in many ways, but they all come down to "meaning." A mentor is equipped to offer practical and specific help to both pre-retiring persons and those already retired. A mentor can use his or her newfound knowledge, skills, and tools in their own parish by offering group and individual consultation, in the immediate community in an evangelistic manner, and to a national and even international audience. A mentor can also use his or her new skills to assist individuals, perhaps friends, church members, community members, family, children, even grandchildren. Some of the necessary qualities of a mentor include being patient, supportive, interested, a good listener, perceptive, aware, self-aware, attentive, and retentive.

Spiritual Mentoring. In their book *Spiritual Mentoring: A Guide for Seeking and Giving Direction* (Intervarsity Press, 1999), authors Keith Anderson and Randy Reese offer a model of spiritual mentoring that is simple yet comprehensive. They begin their discussion with a definition of spiritual mentoring.

> Spiritual mentoring is a triadic relationship between mentor, mentoree, and the Holy Spirit, where the mentoree can discover, through the already present action of God, intimacy with God, ultimate identity as a child of God, and a unique voice for kingdom responsibility. (p. 13)

Spiritual mentoring is not career counseling, psychological counseling, advice giving, pastoral counseling, teaching, disciplining, or confession. Spiritual mentoring is a way to recognize the already present action of God in the mentoree's life. A mentor is anyone who is able to discern the already present action of God in the mentoree. A mentoree is simply one who desires spiritual growth and maturity.

Spiritual mentoring is relational. Spiritual mentoring is based on relationship, a holy union between two people that is ever mindful of the presence of the Spirit as the cohesive force binding them together to each other, to the community of humankind, and to God. This is a relationship characterized by spiritual like-mindedness.

Spiritual mentoring is autobiographical. A mentor can help the mentoree begin to appreciate the panoramic vistas of the mentoree's life and capture their sacred memories. In time, the mentor can help the mentoree start quilting these sacred memories together into a larger tapestry of faith, creating a blueprint for the mentoree's ongoing spiritual development.

Spiritual mentoring is in partnership with the Holy Spiri. The primary task of the mentor is to help the mentoree discover the work of the Holy Spirit. The Holy Spirit has been at work all along; mentors come to recognize and bless this work, helping the mentoree honor this work in new ways. The work of the mentor is not about the mentor; it's primarily about raising the mentoree's awareness of the work of the Holy Spirit.

Spiritual mentoring is purposeful. The mentor seeks to uncover a spiritual life goal, a spiritual dream, a vector of faithful action with the mentoree. Spiritual mentoring helps the mentoree actualize his or her true-life vocation.

Spiritual mentoring requires listening. Listening is not simply hearing the words of the mentoree; it is not even in tracking the concepts, ideas, or points the mentoree is making. Rather such listening is accomplished with the "third ear." This is tuned into the when, where, how, and what of the working of the Holy Spirit in the life of the mentoree.

Spiritual mentoring requires adaptable discernment. Discernment gives the mentor a window of another type through which the genuine motivations and desires of the mentoree become more clearly visible.

Spiritual mentoring belongs to the priesthood of all believers It accepts no boundaries in age, gender, education, intelligence, race, or any other human delineation. God knows no boundaries in offering grace to each and every one of God's children; each child of God is equipped in potential for the ministry of spiritual mentoring. Spiritual mentoring is not the province of the professional, but the domain of all the people of faith. We are all called to reflect the action of God in our hearts, minds, and lives.

MINI-COURSE #13

Finding Peace, Healing, and Wholeness through Spiritual Autobiography

Audience Maturing adults, ministers to maturing adults

Purpose To offer basic information about the importance of spiritual autobiography

Content Once people have been properly educated as to the value and praxis of spiritual autobiography, they almost automatically begin the process. They usually divide into writing groups that meet weekly to share what they have written during the week. What they produce is nothing short of personally profound. They come to see God's presence in their lives in much sharper focus; they grow to appreciate the wonder and delight of the work of the Holy Spirit in every facet of their movement. The very process is motivational, uplifting, fun, and spiritually deepening.

Remembering past life events is a normal, natural, and very healthy behavior that can pay rich dividends. When life remembering is accomplished in an organized and structured manner the process is called "life review." Life review appears to intensify during times of personal change, lifestyle shift, or developmental transition that characterize the maturing years. Life review is not the idle wanderings of a disorganized mind or a means of withdrawing from a disagreeable present. It is not a psychological retreat into wishful thinking of fantasy.

As we become more aware of the value of reminiscing, we can begin actively using it to heighten the richness of our present world. We can grow in our appreciation of the people, events, learning, and relationships we have experienced. We can better understand the unique contribution each has made and gain insight into the patterns of our lives, recognizing the beautiful tapestry that has been woven together with God's hand.

With the clearer vision gained from positive reminiscing, we can take the next developmental step toward personal integration. We come to recognize that behind the seemingly random twists and turns of our life, the invisible hand of God has been continuously at work all along. The celestial artist of all life has been there with us, designing the plan and guiding our progress as our human hand stitched and tucked the fabric, chose and blended the colors, and wove and hemmed the garment to fit us exactly as it should.

In our later years, the pace of making sense of our entire life quickens. Internal and external forces converge, giving us the opportunity of gaining a global perspective of how God has been at work in all the days of our lives. We search for the patterns, themes, successes, and failures that have combined into the amazing amalgam we call our life. In our later years, we arrange the facts of our life into a cohesive whole. We take stock of our life as we never have before. We see new themes, new strands, new waves in our life that we missed in our day-to-day living.

Maturing adults can initiate the process of positive reminiscing in ways that bring them to a personal deepening of faith. Perhaps the best way is through writing. An autobiography of faith starts with our earliest recollections of God-consciousness and proceeds through the decades of our life up to the present. In each decade, we can trace the work of the Holy Spirit in our life as the challenges, successes, failures, and even the monotony of our daily life unfolded to reveal the lessons we encountered in this classroom called life. Writing our chronology of faith stimulates us to catch a glimpse of the grand design of our lives as we continue our life's journey. Our goal is to recognize the lessons of love we have learned. God is the engineer of our life structure; God's hand gives shape to the lessons of our life. Even the losses we experienced as we marched through each succeeding stage of our life ultimately become lessons of love.

Praying: The Heart of the Spiritual Journey

Audience   Maturing adults, all who minister to and with them

Purpose   To offer deeper insights into the importance of prayer in the lives of maturing adults

Content   Prayer is essential for a person of faith at any age, but it becomes even more important as we mature. But even in older age, many people feel confounded by prayer, not really knowing how to pray, feeling inadequate in addressing God and in the very mechanics of the process of prayer. Maturing adults can become proficient in prayer when given sufficient information and encouragement.

Prayer sustains us because it moves us toward our most noble parts and allows us to align ourselves with the Spirit's plan for our lives. Prayer inspires us and gives our life direction that we otherwise wouldn't have. Whatever else prayer does, when done in earnest, it expands our own communion with God. Prayer heightens our capacity for truly understanding our God-given gifts. Our capacity for receiving the grace of God is clearly connected with our prayer life. Prayer gives us a celestial pause so we can detach from the daily routines of life and find spiritual refreshment; it allows us to recharge our spiritual batteries.

Not all that we call prayer is true prayer. True prayer is a genuine impulse of God-consciousness, the knowledge that God is here with us now. Prayer is the mature request for moral growth and spiritual power, a wholehearted yearning to find God. False prayer may be a selfish request for unfair advantage over others. False prayer might also be an angry cry for vengeance. True prayer seeks forgiveness, is based on God's wisdom, and enhances self-control. Prayer equips us with confidence to follow the lead of the Spirit. It gives us courage to face the problems of life by renewing our mind. Prayer seeks new wisdom and energy, it gathers strength for us and offers us better ways of adjusting to the problems of living. In short, prayer deepens our purpose in living. If there is one thing that we need desperately in our senior adult years, it is purpose.

Our primary curing mechanism is medicine, while our primary healing mechanism is prayer. Medicine, in all its forms, serves us well; we use it liberally and intelligently. Likewise, we are called to prayer and especially called in times of trial when we need to be as open as possible to the healing power of God's grace. Although not its primary purpose, prayer may add to the efficacy of medical treatment in many ways. Certainly, prayer has the power to transform our personalities by making us more resilient to discomfort that sickness brings. Prayer is a mighty force for promoting our own health and well-being. Prayer, due to its introspective nature, is a sound psychological process as well as a spiritually uplifting one. Prayer allows us to come to a fuller realization of our own God-given powers and to focus them more clearly on our current situation.

Dr. Larry Dossey has written an intriguing book entitled *Healing Words.* He says that prayer can guide and sustain us so we can courageously confront our trials. Prayer is our primary tool for addressing the fear and anxiety that generally accompanies sickness, especially protracted sickness. Prayer can so vitalize us that the severity of our ailments seem to lessen. Perhaps the most widely used form of prayer is intercessory prayer, where we seek a specific outcome. When we ask God for a cure to our affliction, a remedy for our maladies, or a cessation to our sickness, we are engaging in intercessory prayer. Genuine prayer, however, does not mean "telling God what to do."

> Prayerfulness is accepting without being passive, is grateful without giving up. It is more willing to stand in the mystery, to tolerate ambiguity and the unknown. It honors the rightness of whatever happens…. (p. 24)

> Prayerfulness allows us to reach a plane of experience where illness (and sickness) can be experienced as a natural part of life, and where its acceptance transcends passivity. If the disease disappears, we are grateful; if it remains, that too is reason for gratitude. (p. 27)

Spiritual Gifts Survey for Maturing Adults

I created the following survey to help maturing adults and those who work with them get a firmer grip on their unique spiritual gifts. The spiritual gifts I refer to are described by Paul in his letters to the Philippians, Galatians, and Ephesians.

Directions: Read each statement and determine to what extent it is true for you. Please respond to each and every statement. Place your response (only one number) in the space to the left of the statement number. Your five possible choices for response are:

    4...All the time
    3...Most of the time
    2...More than average
    1...Average
    0...Not at all

_____1.   I like to show acts of kindness to others, especially senior adults so they can see God's powerful love in their lives.

_____2. I seem to be drawn to persons in need of encouragement or an uplifting word.

_____3. I try to help all that I can to assist the church in general and church-sponsored events to operate well.

_____4. I will do just about anything to help others so they can go out and minister to others and preach the word of God.

_____5. I find myself trying to figure out how I can help with the everyday needs of others.

_____6. Even if I'm talking with a stranger, I find that I can get around to mentioning God or the gospels in some way.

_____7. I find myself studying the Bible and other spirituality materials so I can explain them with clarity.

_____8. I feel really good when I know that I have helped a senior adult sort out a problem or personal obstacle.

_____9. I would offer my home for senior adult gatherings from the church.

_____10. I feel that God has given me a special gift and sensitivity in praying for others in various situations.

_____11. I can select the right people to get the job done.

_____12. I look for more efficient ways to get a job done.

_____13. I find it easy to forgive and give a person the benefit of the doubt, to give them another chance.

_____14. I search for ways I can genuinely compliment or affirm others.

_____15. I really like serving others so they can have the most pleasant worship or learning experience at church.

_____16. I like feeling useful by doing everyday tasks for others.

_____17. I enjoy being faithful to meeting the financial needs of my church.

_____18. I have led others to gain stronger spiritual dimensions for their lives.

_____19. I have been told that I have a gift in teaching others.

_____20. I feel a great fulfillment when I can give counseling, guidance, or assistance to others.

_____21. I like to help people in the church feel welcome and comfortable.

_____22. When I pray for others, I receive a special sense of personal meaning and a felt connection with God.

_____23. I find that if I'm going to serve on a committee or board, I'd rather be in a leadership position than not.

_____24. I'm good at organizing and coordinating events, meetings, etc.

_____25. I'm pretty good at picking up on personal cues, especially if a person is hurting emotionally.

_____26. I feel drawn to help people who might be hurting.

_____27. I find myself thinking about what needs to be or could be done to make things run more smoothly around the church.

_____28. I like to reach out to help people who may need assistance of whatever sort so they can get to their own work without worrying.

_____29. I know that God will always meet my financial needs, so I feel confident in giving support of the church's mission.

_____30. I think I have somewhat of a reputation as a person who can fairly easily receive others who need to hear about God.

_____31. I enjoy, or would enjoy, teaching a class or even a session on some spiritual topics.

_____32. I can guide others to relevant scriptural verses that apply to their situation.

_____33. I reach out and try to make newcomers welcome in our church.

_____34. I find it easy to pray for others anytime, day or night.

_____35. I like to take a group through an evaluation process of a task we have just completed so we can discover if there might be a better way of going about it the next time.

_____36. I like to establish systems, procedures, and/or policies so things can run as smoothly as possible.

_____37. Visiting senior adults in hospitals or nursing homes is a rather easy and even personally meaningful activity for me.

_____38. When I can see a senior adult is hurting, I'm moved to offer them comfort and/or encouragement.

_____39. I am naturally drawn to encourage others, especially senior adults in the church.

_____40. I find it uplifting to help senior adults with daily living tasks so their life is a little easier.

_____41. I feel a special call to help the church meet its own financial needs, and help the church meet the financial crises of its members as well.

_____42. I like to talk about spiritual matters with persons who need or would like a closer relationship with God.

_____43. I like explaining points from the Bible, or other spiritual concepts, to senior adults.

_____44. Senior adults feel free to approach me; they know that I care for them as people and as children of God.

_____45. I like to serve others at church suppers and other such events at the church.

_____46. I like to pray for others; I feel my prayers *do* make a difference.

_____47. When in group situations, I am selected to lend leadership or direction to the group.

_____48. I like adding efficiency and effectiveness to the administrative processes of an organization.

NOTE: This Spiritual Gifts Survey for Maturing Adults is a modification of a spiritual gifts assessment form created by Grace Church, St. Louis, Missouri; used with permission.

Spiritual Gifts Survey for Maturing Adults

TABULATION SHEET

After completing the forty-eight questions on the mini-assessment, transfer your responses to the chart below. After all your answers are charted, total these point values by adding downward into the total column at the bottom.

A	B	C	D	E	F	G	H	I	J	K	L
—	—	—	—	—	—	—	—	—	—	—	—
1	2	3	4	5	6	7	8	9	10	11	12
—	—	—	—	—	—	—	—	—	—	—	—
13	14	15	16	17	18	19	20	21	22	23	24
—	—	—	—	—	—	—	—	—	—	—	—
25	26	27	28	29	30	31	32	33	34	35	36
—	—	—	—	—	—	—	—	—	—	—	—
37	38	39	40	41	42	43	44	45	46	47	48
—	—	—	—	—	—	—	—	—	—	—	—

TOTALS

A	B	C	D	E	F	G	H	I	J	K	L
—	—	—	—	—	—	—	—	—	—	—	—

Personal Assesment Study

Indicate the three highest scoring gifts from your *Spiritual Gifts Survey for Maturing Adults* by putting the total point value and alphabetical letter of those gifts in the space provided below. Begin with the highest scoring gift as number 1 and end with the third highest at number 3. Then fill in the title of the corresponding spiritual gift from the chart below.

My spiritual gifts are:

Point Value	*Letter*	*Spiritual Gift Title*
1. _____	_____	_____
2. _____	_____	_____
3. _____	_____	_____

A_____	MERCY
B_____	EXHORTATION/ ENCOURAGEMENT
C_____	SERVICE
D_____	HELPS
E_____	GIVING/STEWARDSHIP
F_____	EVANGELISM
G_____	TEACHING
H_____	SHEPHERDING/PASTORING
I_____	HOSPITALITY
J_____	INTERCESSION/PRAYER
K_____	LEADERSHIP
L_____	ADMINISTRATION

Note: You can find invaluable *Spiritual Development Inventories* (developed by the JOHNSON Institute) on the website www.SeniorAdult Ministry.com. Each of these inventories generates a personal report that allows maturing adults to dramatically advance on their path toward becoming that special, one-of-a-kind spiritual self that God intends for them to become.

Glossary

Ageism: Our cultural fear of the aging process; the fear that our later years may be irrelevant.

Aging services network: The sum total of all the services given by all the agencies and organizations, public and private, for profit or not-for-profit, that are dedicated to the care, well-being, and advancement of senior adults.

Assisted living: A living environment for maturing adults who require some assistance but only minor, if any, medical care. Meals are provided and usually an activity/recreational therapy program is also included.

Boomers: The cohort of maturing adults that generally includes the time of later middle age.

Builders: The cohort of maturing adults that generally encompasses the time from the end of the Boomer stage until the onset of the Elder stage.

Care partner: The individual, in a caregiving relationship, who receives care from the caregiver.

Cohort: An age-graded subset of the population referred to as a group, e.g., Boomers.

Compassion fatigue: The emotional state resulting from over extending oneself in a caregiving relationship, the symptoms of which include mixtures of anxiety-like and depression-like behaviors.

Elder: A person who, by a combination of maturation and experience, has entered a "twilight" time of life where her or his primary function is that of sage.

Parish ministry for maturing adults: The creation and execution of spiritual development, education, and peace- and justice-oriented outreach activities specifically designed to enrich the sacred relationship between the maturing adult and God.

Healing gifts: A range of thirty virtues that have been identified by research to positively affect healing.

Independent living facility: A living environment for maturing adults who require housing. Maturing adults live in separate units. They may or may not be provided meal service and perhaps reminders for medications, etc., but little else.

Intergenerational faith formation: Activities directed at advancing the spiritual and/or faith development of at least two cohorts through and by their interaction.

Intentional ministry: Any predetermined, organized, directed, and objective driven activities, exercises, curriculum, and or evangelical activities that have spiritual development and/or faith formation as its goal.

Learning community, faith-based: A group of people who are dedicated to expanding their minds, hearts, and souls.

Lifelong faith formation: The notion that each phase and each stage of life offers unique spiritual learning opportunities.

Maturing adults: A general term referring to all adults over a certain chronological demarcation. For our purposes here, we divide the larger group of maturing adults into three cohorts: Boomers, Builders, and Elders.

Personal vocation: The notion that each and every person, regardless of age or situation, has at least one unique "work" that is performed primarily because it serves God.

Residential care: A living environment for maturing adults where minor services are offered to the residents, such as medication distribution, linen service, food service, transportation, and other care services.

Senior adult ministry: A term describing a more or less comprehensive approach to faith formation for senior adults.

Senior groups: A term used to describe a parish-based organization whose primary purpose is recreation, fellowship, and socialization.

Skilled care: A living environment for maturing adults who suffer from some sickness. Services provided to residents include all that are provided in residential care, but with the addition of full-time nursing care. Skilled care is what was formerly called a "nursing home."

Spiritual autobiography: A written autobiography that includes the story of the author's faith walk with God throughout their life.

Spiritual gerontology: A sub-discipline of the study of gerontology that focuses on the religious or spiritual aspects of personal growth and development.

Spiritual mentor: A person who assists another to discern the hand of God in their life.

Transformative learning: A type of inner life learning that affects the learner in profound ways and has the effect of reshaping the learner's perspective of and approach to life.

Recommended Resources

Alderman, Margaret. *Each New Sunrise: Meditations in Maturity.* Winona, MN: St. Mary's Press, 1999.

Anderson, K. R and R. D. Reese. *A Guide for Seeking and Giving Direction.* Westmont, IL: Intervarsity Press, 1999.

Arn, Win and Charles Arn,. *Catch the Age Wave.* Kansas City, MO, Beacon Hill Press, 1999,.

Benton, Sharan, A. *Wisdom Keepers: A Resource for Faith Sharing Among Maturing Adults.* Winona, MN: St. Mary's Press, 2000.

Bianchi, Eugene, C. *Aging as a Spiritual Journey.* New York: Crossroads,1992.

Billy, Dennis. *Into the Heart of Faith.* Liguori, MO: Liguori Publications, 1999.

Burke, Mary Thomas and Judith G. Meranti. *Counseling the Spiritual Dimension.* Alexandria, VA: ACA Press, 1995.

Carlsen, Mary Baird. *Creative Aging: A Meaning Making Perspective.* New York: W. W. Norton & Co., 1991.

Chittister, Joan. *Fire in the Ashes; A Spirituality of Contemporary Religious Life.* Kansas City, MO: Sheed & Ward, 1995.

Curry, Cathleen, L. *When Your Spouse Dies.* Notre Dame, IN: Ave Maria Press, 1990.

Dorff, Francis. *The Art of Passingover.* New York: Paulist Press, 1988.

Dossey, Larry. *Healing Words.* San Fransisco: Harper SanFrancisco, 1993.

Dunne, Thomas Aquinas. *Spiritual Mentoring.* San Fransisco: Harper SanFrancisco, 1991.

Felber, Marta. *Finding Your Way After Your Spouse Dies.* Notre Dame, IN: Ave Maria Press, 2000.

Fischer, Kathleen. *Autumn Gospel: Women in the Second Half of Life.* New York: Integration Books, Paulist Press, 1995.

Gallagher, David, P. *Senior Adult Ministry,* Loveland, CO: Group Publishing, 2002.

Gentzler, Richard H. *Designing an Older Adult Ministry.* Nashville, TN: Discipleship Resources, 1999.

Gentzler, Richard H. and Donald F. Clingan. *Aging: God's Challenge to Church and Synagogue.* Nashville, TN: Discipleship Resources, 1996.

Green, Thomas, H. *When the Well Runs Dry* Notre Dame, IN: Ave Maria Press, 1998.

Groeschel, Benedict. *Spiritual Passages.* New York: Crossroads, 2000.

Gunzel, Raymond, J. *The Treasures of God.* Notre Dame, IN: Ave Maria Press, 2002.

Koenig, Harold, and Andrew Weaver. *Pastoral Care of Older Adults.* Minneapolis, MN: Fortress Press, 1998.

Kreeft, Peter. *Love is Stronger than Death*: San Francisco: Ignatius Press, 1992.

———. *Prayer: The Great Conversation:* San Francisco: Ignatius Press, 1991.

Johnson, Richard P. *A Christian's Guide to Mental Wellness.* Liguori, MO: Liguori Publications, 1990.

———. *Body, Mind, Spirit.* Liguori, MO: Liguori Publications, 1992.

———. *Caring for Your Aging Parent.* St. Louis, MO: Concordia Publishing, 1995.

———. *The 12 Keys to Spiritual Vitality: Powerful Lessons in Living Agelessly.* Liguori, MO: Liguori Publications, 1998.

———. *How to Honor Your Aging Parents.* Liguori, MO: Liguori Publications, 1999.

———. *Creating a Successful Retirement: Finding Peace and Purpos.* Liguori, MO: Liguori Publishing, 1999.

———. *All My Days: A Personal Life Review.* Liguori, MO: Liguori Publications, 2000.

———. *Loving for a Lifetime: 6 Essentials for a Happy, Healthy, and Holy Relationship.* St. Louis, MO: AGES Press, 2002.

———. *The Nun and the Doctor: A Conversion Love Story at Midlife.* St. Louis, MO: AGES Press, 2004.

———. *What Color is Your Retirement?* St. Louis, MO: Retirement Options Press, 2006.

Levine, Terri. *Coaching for an Extraordinary Life.* Buckingham, PA: Lahaska Publishing, 2001.

Myers, Jane and Valerie Schwiebert. *Competencies for Gerontological Counseling.* Alexandria, VA: American Counseling Association, 1996.

Regan, Jane, E. *Toward an Adult Church.* Chicago, IL: Loyola Press, 2002.

Rolheiser, Ronald. *Seeking Spirituality.* London: Hodder & Stoughton, 1998.

———. *The Restless Heart,* New York: Doubleday Books, Inc., 2004.

———. *The Holy Longing.* New York: Doubleday Books, Inc., 1999.

Rooney, Linda. *Habits of the Soul: Learning to Live on Purpose.* New London, CT: Twenty-Third Publications.

Rupp, Joyce. *The Cup of Our Life.* Notre Dame, IN: Ave Maria Press, 1997.

Saucer, Bobbie Joe. *Our Help in Ages Past.* Valley Forge, PA: Judson Press, 2005.

Schlehofer, Jo. *Celebrate the Older You.* Notre Dame, IN: Ave Maria Press, 1998.

Seeber, James, J. *Spiritual Maturity in the Later Years.* New York: The Haworth Press, 1990.

Sofield, Loughlan, Carroll Juliano, and Rosine Hammitt. *Design for Wholeness.* Notre Dame, IN: Ave Maria Press, 1990.

Srode, Molly. *Creating a Spiritual Retirement,.* Woodstock, VT: Skylight Paths Publishing, 2003.

Toffler, Alvin. *Future Shock.* New York: Random House, 1970.

United States Conference of Catholic Bishops. *Co-Workers in the Vineyard of the Lord,* document #5-722. Washington, DC: USCCB Publishing, 2005.

———. *Blessings of Age,* document #5-341. Washington, D.C: USCCB Publishing, 1999.

Vann, Gerald. *The Divine Pity.* New York: Fountain Books, 1945.

Viorst, Judith. *Necessary Losses.* New York: Fawcett Books, 1986.

Whitehead, Evelyn and James Whitehead. *Christian Adulthood: A Journey of Self-Discovery.* Liguori, MO: Liguori Publications, 2005.

———. *Seasons of Strength.* Winona, MN: St. Mary's Press, 1995.

Wiederkehr, Macrina. *Gold in Your Memories.* Notre Dame, IN: Ave Maria Press, 1998.

———. *Behold Your Life.* Notre Dame, IN: Ave Maria Press, 2000.

Wicks, Robert, J. *After 50: Spiritually Embracing Your Own Wisdom Years:* New York: Paulist Press, 1997.